# A G ... d
# Running Your Own Company

Easyway Guides

1

ISBN:

978-1-84716-642-5

Printed by 4edge www.4edge.co.uk

Cover design by Bookworks Islington London N1

# Contents

***************

# Chapter 1

## Initial Thoughts-Thinking Through Ideas and Plans

---

It is very important, right at the outset, to have a clear idea of why exactly you want to go into business. Many people have vague ideas of why they want to start a business. Quite often, no experience at all is involved, just a basic desire to either achieve independence, make money, conquer the world or whatever. Achieving independence and making money are laudable goals, conquering the world is not really a goal. More than ever, in this period of one of the worst recessions that we have seen, one needs to be very clear about the reasons for starting a business and to be equipped with the necessary tools to make a go of a venture.

Most often, people will develop businesses from a hobby or a part time activity that expands with time and turns into a business. However, if this is the case, it must be clear that sufficient profit can be generated to earn a living and provide for further expansion.

### Skills required to run a business

Anyone who wishes to start up and run their own business needs to understand that it is very different to working in a nine-to-five job. Working for an employer means that you have the security of an income, pension, defined working hours, protection through legislation and fixed holidays. Not so when you run your own business. Although you have protection through legislation, you cease to be an employee in the traditional sense and you work for yourself. This entails long hours, uncertain rewards and uncertain outcomes. In short you will need to possess qualities that will enable you to run a business. These qualities are:

- Self-discipline and the ability to work hard
- Motivation and enthusiasm
- The ability to withstand pressure
- The ability to make decisions
- The ability to relate to people

When you run a business you no longer work for someone else, with that person taking all the strain but you are now on your own and have to provide the direction for your business and any other people involved in it.

## The nature of your business

Obviously, if you have taken the decision to start your own business, you should have some idea of what it is that you want to do. Maybe you don't, but have picked up this book to give you some ideas.

Most people will be entering the market place with a product that is in competition with others. Quite often, the market place is crowded. In addition, the growth of online business has been phenomenal which further crowds the scene. Whether your business sis offline or online, you will no doubt have a website which serves as a further shop window to the world.

It is very important if this is the case to understand what your Unique Selling Point (USP) is and what competitive advantage you are offering. Are you offering lower prices, a better standard of service or faster response if breakdowns occur? The advantages that you can offer will depend on your business and the type of service.

However, it is important to know that, if you are entering into competition with others, then the only way you can gain any market share is by having an advantage that will appeal to customers and also a clear idea of how you are going to launch your business, where you are going to launch it and who your target group is going to be. These areas will be thoroughly explored as we work through this book.

## The ways of starting a business

There are several ways to start a business. You can start it from nothing, you can buy into a franchise or buy an existing business.

## Starting from nothing

This is possibly the most difficult and certainly the riskiest way of starting a business. You will need to have researched the market thoroughly, know what you are doing, where you are going, have formulated a plan and have finance in place. Money is always tight in the early days and it is vitally important that you don't waste money or take bad advice. A fool and his or her money are easily parted.

The key to initial start ups is to keep things small to start with. Spending money on unnecessary things means less profits and less chance of survival. Only start a business in an area where you have sound knowledge. If you don't you will spend a lot of expensive time learning from your mistakes.

## Looking at Franchises

A franchise is a business relationship between the franchisor who has a tried and tested business concept and the franchisee who will purchase the right to operate this business. A franchise will involve a capital investment and payment of ongoing royalties or management fees based on sales-turnover or as a mark up on goods supplied for resale by the franchisor.

## Advantages and disadvantages of a franchise

The main advantage of buying a franchise is that you will be buying a tried and tested business idea. Although usually not cheaper than starting your own business you are cutting out all the steps to achieving brand recognition. There are lots of benefits to buying a franchise, the main ones being:

- You will be purchasing a business concept that has been tried and tested in the marketplace
- Lower risks in initial set-up
- Business premises will all comply with a blueprint, which satisfies all regulations
- Publicity and ongoing marketing will be supplied by the franchisor as will training and education in the business field
- Networking opportunities will be available with other franchisors
- You will be operating in a defined geographical area.

In addition to the above, gaining funding to start a franchise is a good deal easier (depending on the franchise) than a start up business. In some circumstances, the franchisor may be able to offer funding for the franchise start up.

## The disadvantages

Like most things in life, there are down sides. Once a franchise is purchased, it can be difficult to dispose of it as there are often terms imposed as to resale. Disputes can arise as to the royalty or management fee and there is also the possibility that the franchisor may fail leaving you with a business that may not be viable in isolation.

## Different types of franchise

There are franchising opportunities available for all sorts of businesses. In order to assess whether a business is suitable for franchise there are a number of factor which you need to consider:

- the main one-the original business concept must have been tried and tested and proven to be a success.
- The franchise must have a distinct brand image and tried and tested methods
- Operation of the franchise must be profitable and provide the franchisor with a limit

If you look in some popular papers, such as Daltons Weekly, you can see a whole proliferation of businesses that are for sale as so-called franchises. It is, or should be immediately obvious, that such businesses are highly suspect. It is necessary to look at the characteristics of a business for sale to gauge whether or not it is suitable for franchise. These characteristics will include:

- Products that have a very short life span in the market
- Businesses with minimal profitability
- Business with repeat business based on loyalty to an individual rather than a product or service
- Businesses that are specific to one geographical area.

There are three types of franchise:

- Job franchise-where effectively you are purchasing a job for yourself. These franchises will be one-person businesses and will require you to invest up to £20,000. Examples range from carpet cleaning to vehicle repair.
- Business franchise. Somewhat more complex as these involve the purchase of a complete business with staff. These types of franchise can cost up to £100,000. Such franchises will include fast food outlets and print shops.
- Investment franchises. These are at the top end and usually include hotels and restaurants and a substantial investment will be required, often up to £1 million.

Beware when entering into a franchise. As mentioned there are many 'scams' out there. It is highly advisable to go to one of the franchising conferences, held in the main cities, in order to gain a better idea of what the franchising world is all about.

## Buying an Existing Business

There are many businesses available for sale in all areas of the market and this is, sadly, an area where many people end up losing out, usually to people or concerns that are trying to offload a business that is failing.

## Inspecting a business for sale

If you have identified a business that interest you, it will be necessary to make a number of visits to that business and to carry out a number of 'due diligence' checks. In addition to appraising the business from the standpoint of its operations, such as the flow of customers, attitude of the staff, premises and stock, it is essential that you have a handle on the valuation of the business. Many times business are overvalued and overstate their turnover. It is vital to involve professionals, such as lawyers and accountants at the outset. This may cost but is nothing compared to the cost to you if you buy a business and realise that it is failing.

There will be a number of elements involved in forming the price of a business, such as building and stock. It will be essential to ensure that a correct appraisal is carried out. Are the assets as valuable as they are said to be, i.e. their book value? Is the total turnover accurately stated and is it a realistic appraisal of ongoing year on year turnover. Where are the risks?

You will also need to examine the following:

- Trade debtors
- Trade creditors
- Other creditors
- Any agreements such as hire purchase
  and leases, including leases on buildings
- Bank loans

Basically you will need to ensure that you are not purchasing a risk and that all agreements in place will apply to you when you purchase a business.

Goodwill

There is usually an amount involved for 'goodwill' in a business. This will be the payment for having built up the business and their brand name and their commercial reputation. Extreme care should be taken in this area. The owner will argue that they have spent years building up the business. The counter argument will be that benefits have been taken out of the businesses over the years which have been produced by the development of goodwill. A professional appraisal of this area is definitely needed.

## The process of purchasing a business

When you have been through the process of due diligence, it will be necessary to employ the services of a lawyer who specialises in the sale of commercial properties. This person will draw up a suitable contract of sale, compile a schedule of assets and liabilities that are to be included in the sale and the agreed valuation, search companies house for details of all existing directors and shareholders and other information and complete the necessary forms to register the transfer.

The main message is BEWARE when buying a business and carry out a thorough investigation of what you are buying. Look out for any cover-ups and any likely future risks and make sure, before you enter into the purchase that you are totally committed.

## Starting an online business
## Online v traditional business

There are a number of advantages to setting up an online business as opposed to a traditional business:

- Online is relatively inexpensive to create and maintain a presence

- There is an opportunity, because of the worldwide nature of the web, to attract a wider audience and a geographically targeted audience.

However, all of the ingredients necessary for a traditional business are also necessary for an online business, there are just fundamental differences.

In chapter 11 we will be exploring online business start ups in more depth.

Finally...

This book is designed as a series of steps which will help you to gain a clear idea of the ingredients necessary to start and develop a business of whatever kind. The principles are universal, business planning, business analysis, company type and location, financing and marketing and customer care.

*****************

# Chapter 2

## Getting Your Business off The Ground- Business Planning

---

### What is a business plan?

Before discussing the fundamentals of setting up your business, whether a traditional or an online business, we need to look at the basics as they apply to all businesses. The first area is the business plan.

When answering the question, what is a business plan, it is tempting to say that a business plan is a document which the budding entrepreneur can present to his or her bank manager as a means of assuring the latter of the viability of the proposed business, thereby securing start-up funding.

In a sense, this is true. Increasingly, banks are refusing to finance small businesses, simply because so many have gone bust over the last ten years. Moreover, they are tightening the reins, according to many economic commentators, precisely because such small businesses have not thought about how it is they are going to survive and prosper in what is almost always a very competitive environment; they have not produced a business plan.

It is, however, erroneous to see a business plan as simply a tool for negotiation with the bank manager. A business plan is, above all, a strategic document which assists the entrepreneur to think very carefully about all the aspects of the business that they are getting involved in. A good business plan will illustrate detailed research and evidence around such aspects of business as:

- The product/service; what exactly is it? It may be obvious to you, but unless you spell it out it may not be clear to your customers;
- The market; is there evidence of demand for your goods and services? Is the competition fierce? Are you entering a niche market? Is the market prone to fluctuation for any reason?

*If so, how do you propose to deal with this?*

- Your unique selling point (usp); what is it that makes your goods and services better than those of your competitors? Price? Quality? Anything else?
- Yourself; have you got what it takes to be successful in your line of business? What relevant experience/training have you had? How do you propose to remedy any shortcomings in these respects?
- Online business development; what sort of life span are you putting on the business? What are your ultimate business objectives? Growth? Diversification?
- Capital funding; what level of funding, if any, do you need to start up your own business? How much money can you afford to put into it
- Management and personnel; are you intending to employ other people? If so, what will their roles be? How will they relate to you? Are you aware of the legal and cost implications of employing staff?
- Location and premises; from where do you propose to run your business? Does location matter? What size of premises do you need and what do they cost? Is it feasible and/or desirable to work from home?
- Budgeting; what are your overheads and likely level of income? Is there any scope for price variation in order to cope with increased competition?

- Cash flow; at what points in the year will you face big bills? When can you expect an upturn in sales? What level of overdraft, if any, will you need to service the business?

These are the key questions which any good business plan will address, and it is the process of answering them-and thinking about them-which is most beneficial to the entrepreneur.

## How long must a business plan be?

There are no golden rules regarding the length of a business plan. See the sample plan in appendix 1 to this book. Always, the most important aspect of the plan is the quality of research, evidence and information provided. Needless to say, however, if a business plan purports to cover a long period of time, 10, 20, 30 years for example-it will inevitably entail the provision of more information, thus elongating the size of the document.

Large businesses sometimes have business plans which cover a period of up to 30 years. Small businesses, if they have a business plan, normally cover a period of 2-3 years. In the case of new businesses, it is sometimes a good idea to have a business plan for the first year of trading only, to "test the water" and to review the plan at the end of the first year, producing what might be a more realistic 2-3 year plan, based on the experiences of the first year. As a rule of thumb, however, a business plan should aim to be around 10-12 sides of paper in length, with relevant appendices attached (cash flow forecast, profit and loss forecast, budget calculations etc)

## What resources do you need to produce a business plan?
Large companies producing 20-30 year business plans employ highly qualified accountants and financial experts with highly sophisticated computer equipment to assist them in the drafting of their business

plans. As a consequence, the small independent trader may feel somewhat ill-qualified to produce such a plan. However, it is possible to produce a business plan without expensive equipment and expert advice. In particular, because the proposed business is small, there are less complications which experts would normally deal with.

A business plan can be produced by a small trader if he/she has the following resources and assets:

- time
- commitment
- numeracy
- literacy
- patience

These are all the human resources required to produce a business plan. The only other things needed are a pen and piece of paper!

## Ten Quick Tips on Writing Your Plan

Before we look at setting out clear objectives for a business, there are a few pointers which should be followed when producing a plan. .

## Writing your plan for the reader

The starting point for any business plan should be the perspective of the audience. The questions that you need to ask yourself are:

- What is the purpose of the plan-is it to obtain funding, for example? An investor will need clear answers to their questions, such as will they get a return on their investment.

- Have you carried out market research-is your plan detailed enough-without this detail your plan will not clear the necessary hurdles.

- Do you understand the competition?

- Is the plan detailed enough? Business plans should ensure that the reader has enough information to make decisions on whether to fund you, or whatever it is that you are asking them to do.

- Focus on opportunity-if you are seeking investment in your online business it is very important to describe the investment opportunity. In short, why should an investor choose your business over and above others?

- Ensure that you cover all key areas in your plan-you should undertake research on what a plan should contain. It does no harm to obtain as much specialist advice as possible.

- Do your sums-when you are outlining the costs involved you should pay as much attention as possible to detail. Potential investors, whoever they are, will turn away if the figures do not stack up.

- Create an executive summary-one of the most important components is the executive summary of the business plan. This is a summary of the entire business plan and is usually contained at the start of the plan. If investors like it they will read on. If not they will pass. If there is no summary they will probably not even consider it.

- Review the plan-once you have completed the plan have it independently reviewed. Select a person detached from the process.

- Implement the plan-a plan should always be viewed as a living document and contain specifics regarding dates, deadlines and specific responsibilities.

### *Setting out clear objectives for your business and defining a business strategy*

It is absolutely essential to have a crystal clear idea of what the main objectives for your business are. Business objectives relate to a business as a whole and to what you want to achieve in the short and long term. When forming your business plan you will certainly need to be clear about your objectives.

Short-term objectives will relate to what you want to achieve on an annual basis, over a period of twelve months. Long-term objectives relate to a period (usually) of five years.

It has become commonplace now to set up a criteria against which you can measure the effectiveness of your business objectives. This is known as 'SMART' criteria. Within SMART all the objectives that you set for your business must be:

- Specific
- Measurable
- Agreed
- Realistic
- Timed

The above are self-explanatory and enable a business owner to set clear objectives which can be re-evaluated over time.

*SMART objectives should be set against a clear MISSION Statement.*

## Mission statements

The best way to quantify business statements is through a mission statement. The mission statement is really a vision statement which details the whole point of your business. There are four key components of a mission statement which must be succinct and clear:

- The role or contribution that a business makes-what exactly are you in business for?
- A definition of the business-this should be given in terms of the benefits you provide or the needs that you satisfy. It should not define what you do or what you make.
- An outline of your distinctive competencies-the factors that differentiate your business from the competition. These are the skills and capabilities that are offered by you as opposed to other business in the same field
- The indications for the future-what the business will do in the future, what it can realistically achieve.

A clear and coherent mission statement is written in two parts. In the first part you will outline the industry that you are in and the products that you offer. The second part comprises the business strategies that you will follow to achieve success. A few examples might be:

- We will provide a first class service to all customers

- We will achieve high productivity levels through sound planning, organization and teamwork
- We will generate sufficient profits to ensure ongoing investment in the business
- We will earn high employee loyalty and motivation by respecting their capabilities and their motivation and providing training opportunities
- We will gain recognition in the market for being a highly professional, ethical, quality assured business.

Obviously, the above needs to be fleshed out and thought through but it is the basis upon which the operations of your business will be founded and on which the SMART objectives will integrate in order to ensure that the business moves forward and achieves its goals. Mission statements need to be re-evaluated on a regular basis as there is always the ever-present danger that it will become just a form of words that sounds good but has no bearing in reality.

Taking SMART objectives and Mission Statements further, basic marketing objectives should mesh with both. We will be looking at marketing later in the book.

### Defining your business strategy

As the owner of your business, or one of the owners, you will be responsible for defining business strategy. Strategic management, essentially, has three components:

- Analysis-where are you now and where do you want to be?
- Choice-what options are available to you?
- Implementation-implement your strategy based on the analysis and options.

## Strategic analysis

There are two distinct areas of any business that require analysis:

- The environment
- The resources of the business

## PESTE analysis

There are a number of factors in the environment that can have an impact on your business. The PESTE analysis enables you to focus on these. PESTE stands for:

- P = Political
- E = Economic
- S = Social
- T = Technological
- E = Environment

## Political

When examining the effect of political forces on a business we are really referring to legislation which has a direct impact on business, such as health and safety legislation and employment law. It is necessary to comply with all legislation and to be seen to be doing so.

## Economic

Economic forces will include all the variables that may have an effect on the profitability and sustainability of your business. These can include, inflation, interest rates and, if you trade abroad, interest rates. Changes in the budget will also, invariably, have an effect on you.

## Social

Social forces can be complex and include demographic changes that will affect your business. For example, if you sell shoes, the fact that there is a falling birth rate in a particular part of the country may affect demand, will affect demand, for the type and size of shoes needed over the longer term.

## Technological

The rapid changes in information technology and relevance to all businesses must be taken into account when devising future strategy. Obviously, if you are planning an online business, this is particularly important.

## Environmental

The impact of business on the environment must be evaluated and taken into account when formulating any business strategy.

## Auditing resources

Having considered the business environment through PESTE, we should now look at auditing the resources of the business. If the business is new then an analysis of what resources might be required to achieve your aims will be necessary. There are three main headings under which your resources will fall:

- Physical resources

- Human resources

- Financial resources

## Physical resources

Physical resources include plant, machines, tool, vehicles and so on. An audit of these resources whether existing or needed in the future will include longevity, cost of future replacement and also maintenance. However, as you are an online business, physical resources such as those outlined above may not be a key feature of your operation.

## Human resources

This will be an assessment of staff needed in the future, if you are a new business, or existing staff if you are established. An audit of human resources should take into account staff development, which will be based on the future skills requirements of staff allied to your own strategy for the business.

## Financial resources

This area, like the other two, is of vital importance. Without financial stability the business will not survive. An audit of financial resources will include all the sources of finance that you have. This audit will also include an analysis of debtors and creditors. The end result should be a clear determination of current and future viability and, if problems are identified, the rectification of these problems.

## Strategic implementation

There are two aspects of implementation that you need to consider. One is planning carefully the other is the actual implementation.

There are three key areas into which you can break down the implementation process:

- Planning and allocation of resources
- The structure of the business
- Management of the people and the systems in the business.

## Planning and allocation of resources

The resources of a business, as we have seen, are physical, human and financial. For a new business it should be fairly easy to plan what resources are needed and then allocate them. However, this is more complex for a growing business. The planning of physical and human resources will be easier than the planning of financial resources.

***************

# Chapter 3

## The Structure of a Business

### The legal Structure of Your Business

There are various structures within which your business can operate and it is essential, when formulating your business plan that you understand the nature of each structure.

### The sole or proprietary business

This is a business owned by one person. If you are operating alone then this may be suitable for your purposes. The person and the business are legally one and the same. It does not matter what or who you trade as, the business is inseparable from yourself, as opposed to a limited company, which is a separate entity. All financial risk is taken by that one person and all that persons assets are included in that risk. The one big advantage is that all decisions can be taken by the one person without interference.

A second advantage is that the administrative costs of running a sole business are small. If your business is VAT registered then you will need to keep records, as you will for Her Majesty's Revenue and Customs. However, there are no other legal requirements.

### Partnerships

Partnership is a business where two or more people are joined by an agreement to run that business together. The agreement is usually written, given the potential pitfalls that can arise from a partnership.

Liabilities which may arise are shared jointly and severally and this should be made clear to anyone entering a partnership. Even if you only have 1% of the business you will still be responsible for 100% of the liability. All personal assets of each partner are at risk if the business fails.

Decisions are taken jointly, as laid down by the partnership agreement. If the agreement lays down that partners have differing decision making capacity dependent upon their shareholding then it could be that, in a three way partnership, the decision making process may be hampered because a decision cannot be reached unless the major investor is present.

It is very important indeed to consider the nature of the agreement that you are entering into and it may also be advisable to take legal advice.

Partnership usually reflects the way that business was capitalised although other factors may be taken into consideration. For example, an expert in a particular field may join with an investor to create a 50/50 partnership.

It is very advisable indeed to consider carefully the ramifications of entering into a partnership. Many such arrangements end in tears, with both partners hostile to each other. Personal bankruptcy can occur as can the ruin of the partner(s). Profits are usually shared between partners in accordance with the terms in the agreement.

## The limited liability company

This type of company has evolved over the years and provides a framework within which a business can operate effectively. A limited company is usually the best vehicle for all but the smallest of businesses. It is certainly the only sensible answer if capital is being introduced by those who are not actively involved in running the business (shareholders).

Shareholders inject capital and receive a return (dividend) in proportion to the capital they invest. They are eligible to attend an annual general meeting to approve or otherwise the way the directors are running the business. Annual General meetings also determine how much of the profit will be distributed to shareholders.

Voting is in accordance with the number of shares held and the meeting can replace all or any of the directors if a majority are dissatisfied with them.

Shareholders can, if a majority request, call an Extraordinary General meeting to question directors about performance, outside the Cycle of Annual General Meetings.

Control of the company is in the hands of directors who are appointed by the shareholders to run the company on their behalf.

The company is a legal entity in its own right and stands alone from the directors and shareholders, who have limited liability.

When a company is created it will have an "Authorised Shareholding" That specifies the limit of a shareholders liability. If all shares have been issued then shareholders are not liable for any more debts that the company may accrue.

***************

# Chapter 4

# Patents and Registered designs

In order to grow, industry must continually create and develop new ideas. Innovation is expensive and innovators need protection, to ensure that others cannot pirate their ideas. All of the above items are known as "intellectual property" and, with the exception of copyright, in order to register and protect your intellectual property, you need to contact the patent office. Their address can be obtained from the Chartered Institute of Patent Agents on 0171 405 9450.

## Patents

If you or your company have produced what you consider is a unique product or process, it is very important to register it as soon as possible, before disclosing it to anyone. The granting of a patent gives the patentee a monopoly to make, use or sell an invention for a fixed period of time. This is currently a maximum of twenty years.

## Registered designs

This involves registering what you consider to be a new design. The proprietor must register before offering the new design for sale in the U.K.

## Trademarks

A trademark is a means of identification-whether a word or a logo-which is used in the course of trade in order to identify and distinguish to the purchaser that the goods in question are yours. A good trademark is a very important marketing aid and you are strongly advised to register it.

## Service marks

This register extends the trademark to cover not only goods but also services. If you are running a hotel for example, you can now register your service mark if you have one.

## Copyright

Unlike the other four categories, copyright is established by evidence of creation, and protection is automatic. To safeguard your position, it might be sensible to deposit your work with your bank or your solicitor or send a copy of your work to yourself by registered post. It should be noted that there is no copyright attached to a name or title, only the work itself.

Having given thought to the likely structure of your business, we need now to consider the right location for your business and also questions relating to the employment and management of staff.

*************

# Chapter 5

## General factors

___

### Location of business

In the first instance, a business may be small and the following may not be so relevant. However, as your business grows you might want to address the question of business location and staff.

The important questions to consider are:

- How many square feet of offices/storage space/workshop/showroom?
- How many square feet of employees facilities?
- How much car parking space?
- How much outside storage for deliveries, storage and packing?

If you are uncertain as to what precisely you need, or you feel that the shape of your business is going to alter substantially and in the short term, do not commit yourself to a hefty purchase, or even as much as a five-year lease. Go instead for a temporary solution, while you determine what your long-term requirements are likely to be. Never enter into a lengthy commitment unless you feel that the premises are likely to suit you in the long term. Whether you are buying a freehold or acquiring a lease, take independent professional advice on the value. Hire a surveyor who will tell you whether the asking price or rent is fair. Whatever your business, the cost of your premises is going to represent a major overhead. If you get it wrong, you will go out of business. It is essential to establish that not only can the property be used for the purpose for which you want it, but also that the planning consent will cover any future business development.

## Working from home

Particularly if you are starting a new business, the idea of working from home is attractive. It enables you to keep your overheads to a minimum, allows you to work the long hours necessary in the establishment of a business, and leaves your options open. If the business does not work out, you are not committed to an industrial property. It needs to be recognized, however, that working from home can cause considerable problems.

Strictly speaking, if you plan to run a business from home, almost certainly you will need approval or permission either from someone or some authority. There are two kinds of restrictions which may affect your ability to run your business from home. The first is a series of contractual relationships which you may have already entered into, such as a tenancy or lease. The second is that imposed by local authorities-planning, highways, health and safety.

## Planning permission

If you want to make a significant alteration to your house in order to accommodate your business, you will need planning permission or building regulations approval. This includes building an extension, loft conversion, in fact almost anything except extremely simple alterations.

## Change of use

Local authorities state that consent has to be sought for any change of use. The interpretation of change of use is difficult but what you have to decide is whether what you wish to do constitutes a genuine material change of use of the building. You should make sure that you have insurance to cover your business activity within your home. If you have an accident which occurs as a direct result of your business then your insurance will not cover it.

## Health and Safety at work

Whatever your position in relationship to your premises, i.e., leasehold or freehold, under the terms of the Health and Safety at Work Act You have certain obligations to protect yourself, your staff, your customers and your suppliers. Health and Safety Legislation is very important and attention should be paid to it.

## Inspectors

There are two types of inspector-local authority inspectors and fire authority inspectors. Local Authority inspectors are concerned with premises where the main activities are:

- The sale or storage of goods for retail or wholesale distribution.
- Office activities
- Catering Services
- Provision of residential accommodation
- Consumer services provided in shop premises
- Dry Cleaning in coin operated units in launderettes
- The keeping of wild animals for exhibition to the public
- Fire Authority inspectors

The fire authority requires that a place of work should have a fire certificate, and in order for your business to get a fire certificate, the premises need to be inspected. The fire authority will wish to see that there is adequate provision for a means of escape in case of fire, and the necessary amount of equipment. The Fire inspectors will advise you these facilities are inadequate, tell you how they can be put right and then re-inspect the premises when you have carried out the necessary work.

## Employing People

At first you may be able to run your business by yourself or with help from your family. But if not, as your business expands, you may need to employ people. Before doing this, some businesses may consider it worthwhile subcontracting work. This may be more cost effective in ironing out short term trading highs and lows. However, if you do need to take on employees, then you must do certain things.

## What are my responsibilities as an employer?

You must give every employee a written statement of terms of employment. At the time of publication, by law, all employees working 16 or more hours a week must be given a written statement of terms after they have worked 13 weeks in the job.

This statement must include the following:

- name of employer
- name of employee, job title and description
- hours of work
- pay details, including how often the employee is paid
- holidays
- grievance procedures
- sickness and injury procedures
- pension schemes
- length of notice needed to end employment
- disciplinary rules, including dress and behaviour

## Discrimination and the law

It is against the law for an employer or a would-be employer to advertise a job that in anyway discriminates against race or sex. After taking on an employee, the anti-discrimination laws still apply to all other parts of the employees job, including wages and holidays.

***********

# Chapter 6

## Financial Control

---

In this section, we will consider the importance of financial control within the process of business planning. In particular, we will look at profit and loss forecasting, cashflow forecasting, effective bookkeeping, tax and insurance and raising capital for your business.

### Profit and loss forecasting

A profit and loss forecast is a projection of what sales you think you will achieve, what costs you will incur in achieving those sales and what profit you will earn. Having this information down on paper means that you will be able to refer to it, and adjust it as your business develops. Not all the headings will be relevant to you, so don't worry if you leave blank spaces.

### Cashflow forecast

A cashflow forecast, as the name suggests, forecasts the changes in the cash which comes into and out of your bank account each month. For example, your customers may pay you after one month, whereas you might pay out for rent or insurance in advance. At the same time, you will have to pay for certain costs such as materials or wages and will need to budget for this.

### Preparing a Cashflow Forecast

Remember that a cashflow forecast helps you to evaluate the timing of money coming into and going out of your business. In showing you the "movement" of money it takes full account of the fact that you may often not be paid immediately for work done and, correspondingly, that you may not have to pay immediately for goods and services you acquire. An important purpose of a cashflow forecast is to reveal the gap between your cash receipts and payments. It will show you whether or not, for example, you might need to borrow, and if so, when you are most likely to require additional funds. It is very common for businesses to need more cash as they grow because of the difference in timing of receipts and payments.

## Other Terms

*Working Capita*-Working capital is the term often used to describe the short-term resources used by the business for everyday trading purposes. This consists of:

*Debtors*-these are customers you have sold to in credit, i.e., they owe you money.

*Creditors*-these are your suppliers who you have purchased from on credit, i.e. you owe them money.

*Stock*-this represents the value of materials you have purchased. They may be purchased for immediate resale or they may be in the process of being converted into a finished article.

*Cash*-this can either be the amount of physical cash you are holding or it may be money held in a current or bank deposit account. All of the above have to be carefully controlled if your business is to prosper.

## Over-trading

A problem common to many small and growing businesses is what is described as "over trading". The more sales you make, the more money you will need to spend on funding material and debtors before you are paid for the sales. If your level of sales becomes too high and you do not have the necessary level of working capital to support it, you may simply run out of cash. This can be disastrous for your business and means that a full order book is not the only thing to strive for. Even with a profitable business and a full order book, it is imperative to have enough cash available. Extra finance can help your cashflow and make it easier to avoid the pitfalls of over trading.

## Check your customer's ability to pay

Before you offer customers credit, check that they can meet their liabilities. You may want to take up bank references.

## Set out your terms of trading

Be specific about when you expect payment, for example, 30 days from the date of the invoice and make your customer aware in advance of work that you do.

## Set up a system

Set up a system which enables you to issue invoices promptly and shows you when invoices become overdue.

## Keep clear and accurate records

Inaccurate invoices or unclear records can be one of the main reasons for customers delaying payments. Make sure you send invoices punctually, to the right person at the right address.

## Collect your payment on time

Establish a collections routine and stick to it. Keep records of all correspondence and conversations. Give priority to your larger accounts, but chase smaller amounts too. If regular chasing does not produce results consider stopping further supplies to the customer. If payment is not obtained, don't hesitate to ask a reputable debt collection agency or solicitor to collect the money for you. Your Business activities will consist of selling goods and/or services. At the same time you will have to spend money on behalf of the business, on the purchase or rent of premises, raw materials, equipment, stationery etc. etc. in order to conduct business.

Remember that every business transaction generates a financial transaction, all of which must be recorded in books of account on an on-going basis. It is a fundamental management requirement that this be done on a regular basis, at a minimum once a week. Leave it much longer, and sooner or later an iron law of accounting will come into operation. You will have mislaid a financial record or simply forgotten to request one or issue one. When you do get around to up-dating the books, they won' balance. Unless you can discover the error before the end of the financial year your accountant will be faced with the task of reconciling "incomplete records", which he or she will enjoy because of the professional challenge but which costs you more money for more of his/her time.

What information must be kept?

As a minimum you must keep records of the following: -

i) All the invoices raised (or rendered) on behalf of the business, either when the goods are delivered or the services supplied, or shortly afterwards. An invoice is a legal document and constitutes a formal demand for money. It must provide enough information to identify the business which sent it, who it was sent to, what it is for and whether VAT is payable.

ii) A list of your Sales invoices numbered sequentially.

iii) All Purchase invoices received, and listed i.e. those demands made on your business for the payment of money.

iv) Wages and salaries paid, and to whom; Income tax and NI contributions paid over to the Tax authorities.

v) All chequebook stubs, paying-in slips/books, counterfoils of petty cash vouchers, business bank account statements. Without these you cannot compile your books of account.

vi) A full record of VAT, whether paid by or paid to the business.

## The advantages of a bookkeeping system for your business

a) To provide accurate information sufficient to assess whether you are managing the business at a profit or a loss, or whether the business is solvent i.e. is there enough cash available in the business to pay all the outstanding liabilities on demand? The right information of the right kind at the right time is a vital management tool. Good management means making informed decisions of the right kind at the right time based on information that is true and therefore trustworthy.

b) To provide the information required for correct assessments of VAT and Income Tax, so as to avoid financial penalties (and possibly a suspect reputation) for incorrect and/or late payments. HMRC keep records for seven years, and so must you. Your accountant will need the best information in order to minimise your tax liabilities, unless of course you decide to submit a statement of income to your Inspector of Taxes without recourse to an accountant. In any event the Inspector will require a calculation of your Income from the business in the form of an Income and Expenditure Account for each trading year.

c) To monitor the behaviour of the business over time by reference to financial summaries "at a glance". You don't need to remember for example how many meals were served in your restaurant business say in this year compared with last year. The comparison that matters is the financial one with reference to the value of those transactions.

## How to record the information you need

There are basically four methods of bookkeeping. Which one to choose will depend largely on the type and size of business you have established. Take advice from a business adviser or accountant if you are unsure as to which is the best one for your needs.

### a) Proprietary systems.

These are best suited for sole traders in cash transaction types of business e.g. jobbing builders, market traders or some small shopkeepers. This type of business requires daily record keeping, often including till- rolls for the cash till and offers a simple method of control over finances.

A number of pre-printed stationery systems are available at business bookshops. Select one that allows you enough space to record all that needs recording. Worked examples are set out at the beginning of each book to show you how to keep cash records and the bank position, which can be calculated by following the instructions included. A list of business stationary systems publishers is found at the end of the book.

Cash businesses are more vulnerable than other types for the following reasons: -
i) It is far easier to lose or misplace paperwork. Therefore it is easier to lose control and lose money. Therefore it is more difficult to plan for the future.

ii) It is far more difficult to separate the cash that belongs in the business from the cash belonging to the proprietor.

iii) HMRC pay far closer attention to cash businesses because of the greater scope for "creative accounting" and tax evasion.

To minimise these risks, cash business-proprietors are strongly advised to pay their daily cash takings into the bank by using pre-printed paying-in books supplied by their bank. It is also vital to obtain receipts for purchases made from the takings and to keep them in an orderly fashion.

## b) The Analysed Cash book System.

This is perhaps the most common method used by small businesses selling mostly on credit, with perhaps some cash sales. It relies on the Single Entry system of bookkeeping, where each entry is, as the name implies, made once only, and all entries are made in one book, the cashbook.

The analysed cashbook is the "bible" of the business. It allows "at a glance" analysis because it is arranged on a columnar basis, showing how much has been received into the business, when and from where, how much of each receipt is attributable to VAT and therefore how much is the net amount belonging to the business. All this information is written up on one side of a pre-printed book, the left-hand page, showing all monies paid into the bank on behalf of the business. On the opposite, right-hand page are set out in separate columns details of what has been spent by the business, in other words, monies paid out of the bank, to whom and when.

## c) The Double Entry System

This method of recording accounts relies on ledgers, or separate books of account for each type of transaction. Far greater detail and control are possible using this system. As well as a cash account there is scope for setting up other ledgers such as the bought ledger for purchases, sales ledger, nominal (or business expense) ledger, salaries and so on. It is much easier to monitor how much has been spent over a period of time on each type of transaction, simply by referring to the particular ledger or account, on each of which a running balance is struck. Every transaction is recorded in the major account called the Cash Account and also in the appropriate subsidiary ledger. In this way the Cash Account acts as a "Control" account for all the separate accounts of the business.

The most important feature of this system is the characterisation of all bookkeeping entries as either a "credit" ("he trusts" i.e." the business owes him") or "debit" ("he owes"). The sophistication of this method lies in the use of two entries for each transaction. For each credit entry in the Cash Account there must be a corresponding debit entry for the same amount in a different account. Likewise for each debit entry in the Cash Account there must be a corresponding credit entry in a different account. The key words are "equal and opposite". That way the greatest possible degree of control is obtained.

## d) Computerised Accounting Systems

A wide variety of off-the-shelf packages are available, which rely on single or double entry methods. It may be tempting to invest in an accounts package at the outset, especially if you intend to use other computer packages in the business. It would be most unwise to start using such a package without understanding the principles that underlie them. Businesses have failed because of the familiar - "GIGO" - garbage in, garbage out. Money is the lifeblood of the business so don't turn it into garbage by neglecting an understanding of the what, why and how of bookkeeping.

***************

# Chapter 7

## Raising finance

---

Raising finance for your business can be difficult or relatively easy depending on the viability of your business and its ability to meet repayments and also the nature and type of assets that your business owns. It is true to say that, during this time of recession raising finance is harder than ever. However, you should consider the options below. There are a number of alternatives when it comes to raising finance:

### Investment of own funds

At the outset it is almost certain that you will have to invest some of your own time and money into your business. The investment will be financial, i.e. money which is an injection of your own funds into the business. If you are trading as a limited company this could take the form of a loan to the company or share capital. If you intend to operate as a sole trader or a partnership this will be owner's or partners capital. The non-financial investment will take the form of assets that you already own, such as tools and equipment, or a vehicle. These will need to be valued for inclusion into the firms records and an accountant will almost certainly need to be employed to ensure that they are correctly valued and comply with relevant guidelines.

### Short-term finance
This type of finance is usually referred to as working capital finance. It is used to finance working capital and pay creditors and is then

itself repaid following receipts of funds from debtors. The most common type of short-term finance is provided by banks in the form of an overdraft.

## Trade credit

Obtaining credit from suppliers is also a type of short-term finance. The terms of credit with a supplier will vary according to the type of your business and the particular supplier.

## Factoring

Factoring services have been used increasingly by small businesses in the last ten years or so, particularly those businesses who work for large companies or corporations who tend not to pay invoices for up to six months. Factoring enables you to bridge the gap between sending out an invoice and receiving payment. Factoring invoices has the advantage that you can receive immediate payment against an invoice, usually around 80% of face value. It has the disadvantage that there is a cost attached to it and it also has a stigma attached to it and can unsettle those with whom you do business with as it is perceived that you have cash flow problems.

## Invoice discounting

This operates on broadly the same principle as factoring but with several differences:

- Control of the sales ledger is retained by you and it will be your responsibility to chase bad debtors, unlike factoring where the bank concerned (usually a bank) will undertake this function

- Because control is retained by you the existence of the arrangement won't be evident to customers

## Long-term finance

If the finance is to be used to purchase any fixed asset then you must obtain long-term finance. It is good practice to raise the finance based on the life cycle of that fixed asset.

## Business loans

Business loans can be raised from a number of sources. The usual source will be your bank if you already have a business account. However, here I must reiterate the importance of a credible business plan as this will be the tool that will persuade the bank manager that you are worthy of a loan. Some loans are secured and some are unsecured. With all forms of business loans you need to know exactly what the terms are. Most loans are from £1,000-£1million and are repaid from 1 year to 20 years. You should consider the merits and demerits of fixed rate loans and variable loans. This will be influenced by the economic climate currently prevailing.

## Grants

If you are looking to secure a small amount of money, a grant or combination of grants may be more suitable for your business. This is one of the cheapest forms of finance but be aware of the non-financial conditions that may be attached to the grant. These could be the number and types of people employed and restrictions on what the money can be spent on. Grants range from local initiatives run by local development agencies to Business Link funding as well as private funds across the country.

There are many thousands of sources of grants and it is not possible to cover them all here. For example, the Enterprise Advisory Service's main database govgrantsglobal.com usually contains over 3,000 sources at any one time. They can, however, be grouped into three categories.

## European grants

The European Union is a huge source of funds for businesses of all sizes and the money is usually distributed through the European Commission. This body administers a number of schemes through what are known as Structural funds. There are also specific grant schemes such as businesses involved in agriculture for example.

## National government

Grants for small firms come from both the UK government but also the Scottish Parliament, Welsh and Northern Ireland Assemblies. Each of these has its own departments and agencies, which hand out the money based on its own criteria and objectives. There are over one hundred of these bodies but among the most important are:

- Department for Business innovation and Skills www.bis.gov.uk
- Department for Employment and Learning www.delin.gov.uk
- Department for Environment, Food and Rural Affairs www.defra.gov.uk
- Industrial Development Board www.bis.gov.uk
- Scottish Executive www.scotland.gov.uk
- Welsh Development Agency wales.gov.uk
- Enterprise Ireland www.enterprise-ireland.com

## Local

In addition to the many local government authorities, there are a number of locally based agencies and organisations which have been established specifically to support and encourage enterprise at a local level. One such example is Business Link which has a grants and support directory where you can search grant schemes by sector or location. www.businesslink.gov.uk

## Eligibility for grants

Each grant scheme has its own set of criteria to determine whether a firm or project is worthy of its money. There is no business or industry sector which is excluded from applying for funds. The vast majority of schemes apply without major restrictions but on those that do eligibility tends to fall into three main categories: location; size and industry.

*Location*–the UK is actually divided up into four countries and in addition to those schemes offered by the UK national government, and those from Europe, each of these four areas has awarding bodies and donates funds to businesses located within their borders.

On top of this, there are a number of 'special areas' across the UK which are specified by the awarding bodies themselves and can be drawn up just for one particular scheme.

Certain areas within the UK also qualify for funding because they satisfy criteria for special assistance drawn up by the European Commission on National Regional Aid which breaks down Europe into tiers 1,2 and 3. The main form of aid in these areas is Regional Selective Assistance, a discretionary grant aimed at safeguarding and creating jobs and increasing regional prosperity.

As you can see there are a plethora of grants. A good starting point to research grant giving bodies is the Enterprise Advisory Service www.arcweb.com. There are a number of other useful websites such as business link, as detailed above.

***************

# Chapter 8

## Products/Markets/Pricing

The area of marketing is, without doubt, one of the most important areas of a business and the one which is usually neglected. Research and analysis of your potential market, whatever you are making or offering, and however you are choosing to sell it, online or offline, is absolutely crucial to the success of your business.

Without customers to buy your products you cannot survive. With any marketing strategy, there are a number of questions that need to be answered at the outset:

- Who are the potential customers?
- What do they buy and why do they buy it?
- When do they buy and where do they buy?

The above questions are not exhaustive but are the key questions when carrying out initial research. Also important is the nature of the customer, how old, occupation, standard of education and income and family position, i.e. married, single, children and also their location. All these are important factors and research should help to shape your business plan. Although this type of market research might seem too heavy initially, it will prove invaluable as your business develops.

## Segmenting the market place

There are a number of different ways to segment customers and markets. There is no one perfect method.

## Geographic segmentation

This is a simple form of segmentation and is relatively unsophisticated, consisting of dividing your market on the basis of geographical location of potential customers This is fine if all sales are made within one particular market. For example, if you are selling in the UK then you can segment customers by region.

## Demographic segmentation

Demographic segmentation is a more sophisticated way of segmenting customers as it involves identifying potential customers according to specific variables such as age, sex, family size, income or lifestyle. There are two main methods used to provide the different socio-economic groupings, the first classifies occupation and social class groups the second, known as ACORN (A Classification of residential Neighbourhoods) classifies types of neighbourhoods.

## Occupation and social class

Here groups are segmented into 6 classes, A to E. Each one denotes a social class type as follows:
A = Higher managerial
B = Intermediate management
C1= Supervisor/ lower management

C2= Skilled manual

D = Semi-skilled/unskilled

E = Lowest level of subsistence

However, when making assumptions about social class, care and skill is required as many assumptions such as disposable income may not be accurate.

## ACORN

This method analyses people, or households, on the basis of the type of property. The information is derived from the census, undertaken every ten years with the last one undertaken in 2011. This system is based on the assumption that consumer lifestyles and behaviour are closely related to neighbourhood types.

Again, an alphabetical system is used, A to K, as follows:

A = Modern family housing for manual workers

B = Modern family housing for higher incomes

C = Older housing of intermediate status

D = Poor quality older terraced housing

E = Rural areas

F = Urban local authority housing

G = Housing with most overcrowding

H = Low income areas with migrants

I  = Students and high status non-family areas

J  = Transitional high status suburbia

K = Areas of elderly people

## Product segmentation

This is a simple form of segmentation which is used to identify people who would buy, or potentially buy, a particular product.

## Benefit and lifestyle segmentation

This takes demographic segmentation one step further by linking the lifestyle of consumers to their decision to buy a particular product. The next step is to differentiate their product, either on quality or other claimed advantages. As we all know, quite often one product is the same as another. However, the manufacturer will differentiate his or her product by branding and association. Different groups will respond to different messages, such as the ability of toothpaste to prevent tooth decay and to whiten the teeth and so on.

## Competitive advantage

This is critical to all marketing. Businesses must differentiate their products from each other in order to gain market share. Competitive advantage can consist of either lower product prices or a better service than competitors. It is crucial that you understand your competitors if you are to obtain a competitive advantage. It is very important that you have as much information about your competitors as possible. You need to:

- Establish exactly who your competitors are
- Identify their marketing objectives
- Analyse their marketing strategies.

You should also look at whether they have any strengths and weaknesses. You can analyse their strengths and weaknesses, and also your own, by carrying out a SWOT analysis. SWOT is the acronym for Strengths, Weaknesses, Opportunities and Threats. A SWOT analysis is compiled using a grid to enable you to consider how you will match your strengths to your opportunities and how you can overcome your weaknesses and threats. Strengths and opportunities are listed in the left hand column and weaknesses and threats are listed in the right column.

(See overleaf)

| Strengths | Weaknesses |
|---|---|
| Something that you are doing well or are good at. It could be a skill, competence or competitive advantage that you have over your business rivals. | Something that, by comparison to your rivals, you do poorly. This is a position that puts you at a disadvantage. |
| Opportunities | Threats |
| Look for realistic growth opportunities in the business | This is a factor that could lead to problems within your business and subsequent decline. |

## Unique selling points (USP)

This is a crucial element in defining the competitive advantage of your business. Identifying your Unique Selling Points will help you define what it is that makes you different from your competitors. You can use

USP's in your marketing. There are a number of questions that need to be asked when identifying USP's:

- Will the customer perceive this as an advantage?
- Is it very different from what my competitors are offering?
- Will customers receive some benefit from the USP?
- Will the USP motivate customers to make a purchase?

Obviously, an advantage (or perceived advantage) must offer and give benefits over and above your competitor's products.

Within all markets there are a number of factors that will be critical to your success. Examples of critical success factors will be delivery time, speed of service, quality of the product and competitive pricing. Critical success factors will vary from industry to industry and market to market. There is no clear formula as to what will be important and crucial to you. It is vital that you identify your own critical success factors.

Pricing Your Product

A well thought out pricing plan is essential to the future prosperity of your business, and will also help you to make the most of your opportunities.

To develop the right pricing plan for your business, you need to start by working out what your costs are. You need to look at what your competitors are charging and try to estimate what your service or product is worth to your customers.

By knowing what costs you are incurring, you will be able to work out what your "break even" point is. How much do you need to sell before your business covers all its costs, including your own (essential) drawings, but before it makes a profit. Unless you can identify what your break-even point is, you could operate at a loss, without realising until it is too late.

Your Costs

Costs can be divided into fixed (overheads) and variable (direct) costs. Fixed costs include your essential personal expenses, such as mortgage, food etc, as well as rent, heating and lighting wages and interest charges. They tend to stay the same no matter how much you sell. Variable costs, however, increase or decrease according to your level of sales.

The most obvious cost here is the actual cost of materials required to manufacture the product but can include other things such as transport, postage or additional labour. The price you charge for your product has to cover all of the variable costs and contribute towards your overheads.

Outlined below is an example of a break-even point.

| Fred Peters Car Wash Ltd | Cost per Annum £ |
|---|---|
| Personal Drawings | 10,000 |
| National Insurance | 294 |
| Tax | 500 |
| Stationary | 100 |
| Advertising | 400 |

| | |
|---|---|
| Telephone | 320 |
| Depreciation of Van (over 5 years) | 1,000 |
| Petrol | 900 |
| Servicing | 300 |
| Road Tax Fund | 130 |
| Insurance | 320 |
| Business Insurance | 140 |
| Materials | 200 |
| Depreciation of Equipment | 200 |
| Bank Loan £3,000 @ 12% | 200 |
| Bank Charges | 100 |
| Accountants Fees | 300 |
| TOTAL | £15,404 |

Fred's essential personal drawings to cover his family expenses is £10,000. He operates a small car wash. He expects to work for 46 weeks a year, allowing for holidays, sickness etc. He estimates that he will work 38 hours per week.

*His annual output is therefore:*

46 weeks a year Times 38 hours times 0.5 cars per hour = 874

His break even point is

$$\frac{15,404}{874}$$

= £17.62 per car

After researching the market in his area, Fred believes he can confidently charge £20 per car, which will give him a reasonable profit.

## Competitors Prices

Unless your service or product is much better than others on the market, you would be unwise to charge a price which is too far above your competitors, as you will find sales very hard to achieve. On the other hand, a low price often implies low quality or low standards. Competing on price alone is a poor option. It is especially important for small businesses to differentiate themselves by other means, such as personal service, convenience or special skills. Customers rarely buy on price alone and it is worth remembering that you can more easily reduce your prices than put them up.

If, when you work out what your prices should be, they do not cover your costs-look again at how you might make your business viable. For example, could you reduce any of your variable costs, could you get supplies more cheaply, can you negotiate a discount or find an alternative supplier? On your fixed costs, could you trim any other expenditure?

Think again about what you are offering. Could it be improved and sold at a higher price? Can you sell different products for more money to increase your profits? Would sales increase if you put up your prices and spent the extra income on advertising and promotion?

Every cost incurred in running your business must be recovered either by what you charge for your time, or by the amount you charge for your products. Profits will be made only after all of your costs have been covered. But you may decide to use different prices in different situations. For example, a plumber offering a 24 hour service might decide to charge a premium rate for his services if he is called out during the night to deal with an emergency, a different rate for weekends and another rate for normal working hours.

Achieving a range of prices for the variety of skills offered, taking into account the time you would be likely to spend on each job and the convenience factor your customers can give you the flexibility to stay competitive, yet still provide a satisfactory income.

***************

# Chapter 9

## Marketing

The next step in developing your business is to look at sales, and how you are going to achieve them which in turn means looking at the market and considering the most appropriate form of market research. Sales are vital to any business. Whatever you produce, you must be able to sell. This is necessary in order to survive. This chapter covers traditional forms of marketing and also techniques used in online marketing.

You must be satisfied that there is a demand for your proposed products and you must be able to determine how you can investigate the market in which you want to operate, how many potential clients there are in either the catchment area you operate in or the wider area. If you work in publishing for example then clearly the market for your product would be different for that of a baker or butcher or plumber. A lot of thought needs to be given to this area.

### Market Research

The tool that is used to determine demand for a product is market research. Market research can be cheap and simple or highly complex depending on how you approach it and what you might want to find out.

Market research, or effective market research should be able to provide you with information as to what people want and also how much they want and what they will pay for it. Competition which might exist should also come to light.

You should not be put off by competition nor should you believe that because there appears to be no local supplier that what you produce will sell. No supplier may mean no demand and competition may mean established demand.

The concept behind all market research is simple-the practice is often not and unless you have a lot of money the costs may be prohibitive. A good example might be a supermarket.

A potential supermarket would want to know concrete facts in order to establish demand. For example, in terms of the percentage of the population, the average number of visits made to a supermarket each year. This they may well be able to establish from their own records if they are part of a chain.

Secondly they would want to know, what distance people are prepared to travel in order to visit a supermarket. This will vary a lot but they would be interested in establishing a national average.

With these two facts the supermarket can then establish the catchment area population for the proposed supermarket. Now they need to know something about the competition. How many supermarkets are there in the catchment zone which might have an effect on the proposed supermarket? This is easily established. However, more difficult to determine is the effect on your potential business. If we suppose that the supermarket decides that only 30% of the catchment area is exposed to competition and that they expect that 50% of that 30% would continue to use the supermarkets they presently use. This means an adjustment to predicted customer base.

However, competition comes from other shops not just supermarkets. This is why calculations are based on average figures since this additional competition will be fairly standard throughout the country. A survey will be carried out in the locality to check that there are no special factors to consider-special factors which may cause adjustments to the predicted customer base either way.

The next question to be considered is; what is the average spend per visit per customer? Supermarkets will almost certainly be able to answer that one from existing records.

From this data, they can predict gross sales and so the net operating profit. If this is not high enough to justify the expenditure, they might be reluctant to proceed with siteing a supermarket.

The above is a simple model and does not take into account a number of complications but it does give an idea of how market research is carried out. There are two very important factors to be considered-average conditions in the industry and catchment area population, or a knowledge of that population. Although the example given covers selling to the general public the same principle applies when considering selling to other business.

It may be possible to determine industry averages by approaching trade associations. A visit to the bank is also very worthwhile as most high street banks keep statistics which they would be willing to make available. A further source of statistics might be a major supplier in an industry.

Somewhat easier is to determine the magnitude of the target market. Businesses generally fall into one or two categories: those where the customer comes to the business to place the order and those where the business goes to the customer to get the order.

In the first category, the size of your target market will be a percentage of the local population. The size of the population can be found by contacting the records office at your local authority. The percentage which applies to your proposed business will be far harder to determine. The classic method is simple-ask a large enough sample to provide an accurate picture. This is easier said than done. A great deal of research experience is necessary in order to be able to design a questionnaire which can elicit all the right information.

If you can afford it, you could consider employing a market research agency to assist you. If you cannot afford it then you should spend time considering exactly what you want to ask and what you are trying to establish. There are many other places which will hold the sort of information you might need. Your local training enterprise agency (TEC) or the trade association relevant to your business will be only too pleased to assist you.

Once you have established your target market, you might wish to consider exactly how you sell to that market. Easy if you have a shop in the middle of a busy shopping area, at least easier than if you produce books and have to cast your net far wider. It might be useful at this stage to look at marketing in a little more depth.

## Bringing people's attention to your product

You have carried out some form of research and now you are in a position where you wish to bring to people's attention your product. Obviously different media are more suited to some businesses than others.

Marketing covers a whole range of activities designed to "identify, anticipate, and satisfy customer needs at a profit" (Chartered Institute of Marketing).

Three questions need to be looked at:

- When do customers want needs satisfied

- How do the customers want the need fulfilled

- How much are the customers prepared to pay for that fulfilment

Having found the answers to those questions we have to decide how best to communicate to the target market our ability to meet their needs at a price that they can afford-and communicate that ability to them at a price that we can afford.

There are various options that we can consider. However, some of these options are expensive and may well not be within our reach.

## Advertising

Advertising takes various forms. It is exceedingly difficult, unless you have deep pockets, to try to deduce the real effectiveness of whichever form of advertising you decide to employ. For example, is it cost effective to spend £800 on a small advert in a tabloid for one day if that £800 could be spent on something longer lasting.

Advertising hoardings and posters are one way. These tend to cover not only billboards but also tubes trains and buses. Hoardings are seen repeatedly by a wide and ever changing audience in the locality of your choice. They are usually inexpensive.

Leaflets

Leaflets can be distributed on a door-to-door basis (either to other businesses or to individual residences) or they can be given to individuals in the street. However, leaflets can also be thrown away as many see them as junk mail. The result is that leaflets tend to have a low strike rate. Leaflets can also be delivered as inserts in magazines and newspapers. Magazines direct leaflets to specific audiences and newspapers to local areas. Both can prove expensive and again will be discarded more often than not.

A more effective use of leaflets is to have them available in places where the target market will see them. The classic case here is for businesses offering non-residential facilities for holidaymakers. These can usually be found in hotels and guesthouses.

Another use of the leaflet is that of a poster in a newsagent or on other notice boards. This can be effective when being used to attract a defined group of the population who gather together in one place where leaflets cannot be made available. Universities or schools might be a good example.

## Directories

Directories will fall into two categories-local and trade. Local directories such as yellow pages are well known mediums of advertising and they are reasonably priced, sometimes free. However, the effectiveness of such advertising depends on what you are doing and also where the ad is placed. Some businesses tend towards directories such as Thompsons because they have less advertisers and are cheaper.

Trade directories are different by their nature. They are unlikely to benefit new businesses as they can be expensive and are in some cases, nationally distributed.

This is of little use if your business is local, of more use if your product is distributed nationally. There are now a number of local area and regional directories, often produced by trade associations. Some are available as a book or on disc for use with computers. Those who subscribe to the disc system often receive monthly or quarterly updates.

## Advertising in magazines

Magazines fall into three categories-general national, local or specialist. Magazines tend to be more expensive to advertise in than newspapers but can be more effective. Magazines have a longer life expectancy than newspapers and are often passed on to other readers. Specialist magazines are read by specific people who may form part of your desired target audiences. It is worthwhile bearing in mind that most magazine are national.

## Newspaper advertising

National newspapers can obviously reach a lot of people but also tend to be expensive. They are also of little value to those offering local services. Local newspaper advertising can be more effective and also cheaper. Free newspapers are cheaper but can be less effective as they also tend to be seen as junk mail.

## Television advertising

It is highly unlikely that television advertising will be relevant in the early years of a business. To launch a television advertising campaign is very expensive indeed. Therefore, this medium will only be a consideration later on, if at all.

## Radio advertising

This form of advertising would only be effective if there are sufficient numbers of listeners in the target market. However, in the right circumstances it can be useful and relatively inexpensive. Timing is very important in this medium as you need to target your slots at the most appropriate times and on the most appropriate programme for your intended target audience.

## Using an advertising agent

Whether or not an advertising agency is employed will be a matter for the individual business concerned. This decision is down to cost. All businesses placing advertising should set an advertising budget. It could be that placing part of your budget with an agent proves far more cost effective than designing your own campaign. Agents are usually good at designing and placing adverts and can negotiate discounts with various media. It is certainly worthwhile consulting an agent in order to get an idea of what they can do for you, at the same time raising your own awareness of the direction you should be taking.

## Direct mail

Direct mail falls into two categories: untargeted or blanket mailing or targeted. Targeted mail is usually far more effective as untargeted mail can be very expensive and also wasteful. Existing customers of a business are well defined and easily targeted. The secret with direct mail is to keep it short, simple and do it as often as is necessary.

## Using sales representatives or agents

Whether or not you choose to use representatives or agents will depend on a number of factors. Where there are few sales required and the selling of a good is complex there may be the need for a representative. Where the product is simple and can be described in an advertisement or leaflet it is unlikely to be necessary to use a representative. There are two main types of representation, the representative or agent.

The representative is a paid member of staff who may or may not receive a bonus or commission based on results. All the representatives running costs will be borne by the business. An agent is a freelance who meets his or her own costs and is paid only on results.

The advantage of using the representative is that he or she uses their entire time devoted to your business and is under your total control.

The agent costs little to run. However, he or she is not totally dedicated to your business. If other products are easier to sell he may ignore yours altogether.

As you can see, there are a number of ways to reach your target audience, once that target audience has been defined. A lot of thought needs to be given to market research and marketing. All too often, they are the first areas to go through the window in search of savings or simply because you are too busy. However, well defined marketing can produce corresponding increase in profits and a clear strategy is an essential part of any business plan.

## Internet Marketing

Having looked at more traditional ways of advertising a business, all of which are relevant, it is now time to look at the process of Internet marketing.

Each business has its own overall budget and also goals and targets. In the ideal world it would be nice to be able to invest in both offline and online marketing. However, the reality for most businesses, particularly start-ups, is that funds are limited. In this case, it is crucial to understand the techniques used in online marketing.

## Search engine optimization

Most users of the internet will begin the buying process with a search engine. Search engines are enormously powerful and therefore it is essential that your website is built, maintained and updated to be both customer and search engine friendly. Effective search engine optimization is about making your website visible to the search engines, primarily Google.

## Making your site visible to search engines

Your site has to be seen to be ranked. Google uses software called Googlebot to scan individual web pages on the internet and what it finds has a direct impact on how thoroughly your site is indexed and how it can rank in the natural Search Engine Results Pages (SERPS).

## Quality content

Good content is the key to a good website. Good content will sell your product. Good content will mean that more and more users will visit your site and become consumers of your products and services. In addition, if you have good content then other websites will want to link up to your site therefore increasing the flow of traffic. If your site and its content is seen as good by Google then it will be ranked higher. People looking for a specific good or service will go straight to your site, bypassing the competition. However, in order to ensure that this is the case, your site should be well designed and regularly maintained and updated.

A by-product of creating good content on your website is that other websites will want to link to your content. This can only be good because it puts your website in a position of being an authority on your given product or service. It will result in more traffic to your site and will attract the attention of Google, improving your rankings. It is no good developing a site which looks attractive and then not maintaining it or trying to optimize your rankings. This will set you back and if you are relying more on people finding your site, as opposed to the more traditional forms of marketing, then it is essential to have an ongoing plan for updating and promoting your site.

## The use of key words and phrases

You will want to find your main, or niche, keywords and concentrate on writing content to exploit the words. Keywords are the tool through which those who search the web find your unique product. If you are selling bathrooms for example you will want to come up with as many associated words as possible such as 'designer bathrooms' or 'Victorian bathrooms' in other words try to differentiate and provide as many entries as possible for the user. To just use the word 'bathroom' will severely limit the access to your own site.

## Search engine marketing

SEM, Paid Search or PPC advertising is a broad subject that will require research on your part to ensure that you know what you are doing before you invest heavily.

SEM allows you to display an advert on the Search Engine Results Pages or the Search Engines network of publisher websites which you can target to display only to users searching for specific keywords or phrases related to your business. You control your account totally, from the text or images of the advert to how much you wish to spend.

If you elect to run PPC adverts with Google, then your ads will be displayed above and to the right of the organic or natural search results, i.e. the sponsored area. Google calls its program Adwords, which is where the search engine makes most of its profits. There are a number of reasons why search engine marketing is effective:

- It is quick to get started
- You are in control of what you spend
- Your campaigns give you instant visibility

What Google has done with Adwords is to create an online auction for every keyword and phrase in every language. The more competitive a keyword, the higher the price. This is how Google makes its money. You should start your Adwords campaign with a small budget, dip your toe in the water, to see how you go. Setting up an account is simple enough and you should ensure that you read the help and FAQ's on the site before committing yourself.

Adwords works by charging you a fee every time someone clicks on your advert-the more you are willing to pay in comparison to others bidding for the same keywords and the better your landing page is (Quality Score) the higher up the sponsored links you will be placed. The bigger your budget, the more users will be shown your advert and the more that will click through. As soon as your budget has been spent, your advert is taken off until the next day. This allows you to keep tight control of your marketing spend and allows you to see very quickly if the campaign is working and to measure the return on your investment.

## Purchasing traffic

When you enter into Google Adwords or place a banner ad on another website you are in effect buying traffic to your site. There are some unscrupulous companies around that charge you for delivering visitors to your site and then don't deliver.

Legitimate performance marketing companies do exist and they are well aware of the business need for traffic. They are also quite sophisticated and can direct the right sort of traffic to your site. Performance marketing companies invest heavily in building up their own network of users or publisher's websites which they then exploit by showing their advertiser's (your) sales message to their network. By carefully categorizing and segmenting their user base, they can effectively ensure that your pages are shown to relevant users. If someone wants law books for example they will only show your advertisement to those interested in law books.

Depending on the size and nature of the performance marketing company you can specify the countries in which you want your advert to be shown or even the approximate age or gender of the target audience. The more specific your requirements the more you will be charged for the service. However, because it is performance based, you will only pay when the campaign results in a conversion.

The following are a sample of companies that offer Performance marketing.

Burst www.burstmedia.com
DoubleClick www.doubleclick.com
www.conversantmedia.com

And there are many more!

## Email marketing

Email marketing is an effective way to send your message before you have had a chance of building up your own database of customers. Performance marketing companies will provide lists that are segmented by interest. You will need to check with the provider that all addresses have been cleared and have given their consent to receive third party promotional emails. I receive many such emails every day which I have not consented to and which I delete, so it is important to do your homework beforehand.

## Affiliation (as advertiser)

There are a wide variety of affiliation networks available which marry advertisers to publishers. Most networks charge new advertisers a set-up fee which gives your business access to the network of affiliates. Set-up fees can be hefty so you need to go into this with care. In addition, most networks charge advertisers a monthly fee which covers continued access to the network. Ongoing performance can be monitored through the networks portal and affiliates reports can be generated. The strongest aspect of affiliation is payment on performance. You only pay a commission if your affiliate delivers a lead, registration or sale. You are free to pay as much or as little as you want for each of these conversions. Affiliates take campaigns seriously and invest time, money and effort to promote advertiser's products and services. The relationship is two way and you also have to be serious, keeping them up to date with new products, pricing and any offers or promotions that you intend to run. As with all aspects of business, good communication is the key.

## Using vouchers and coupons

The use of vouchers and coupons to promote and sell products, usually at a discount, is becoming increasingly popular with online business. The idea has been around for ever, being used for all sorts of offline business but it is now being used for online trading.

Coupons usually allow customers, whether existing or new, to benefit from a promotion by entering a code online at the point of purchasing. The utilization of the code will modify the customers order in some way corresponding to the offer.

These coupons can be printed and distributed through print media, handed out in the street as a flyer or as part of promotional literature, or through any other medium. they can also be distributed online by adding the coupon to a social media post such as facebook or twitter. They can also be sent to existing customers in a mailshot.

The use of coupons as part of your selling strategy will require some work to your site and again this is what you will be asking your web designer to do for you.

## Co-registration

Co-registration is a lead and customer acquisition strategy used by numerous brands. It is performance based-you only pay on results. Co-registration involves placing a short text or image advertisement for your company on the registration pages of high volume third party websites or landing pages. Usually, you are sharing the page with other advertisers who sell similar products or services, or the page is themed in such a way as to link the advertisers. This method of promotion allows users to request additional information about your product or service and in turn provides you with their contact details.

Co-registration allows you to build a permission based, targeted database of consumers interested in your service and, depending on the volume of the third party site, allows you to develop lists very quickly.

## Rich media

Rich media is, basically, videos, pod casts and other images which will serve to improve your visibility and differentiate you from other sites selling similar products. Most shop windows have excellent displays and lure customers in. Web portals should be the same and a short video can do wonders when it comes to displaying your product, or telling customers more about you and your company and what products or services you sell.

## Social media

Social media, such as Facebook and Twitter is now so widespread that it would be foolish not to advertise your existence on their sites. By opening accounts with platforms such as Facebook, Twitter and Linked In you will be able to reach your potential audience and also hear what is being said about your company, product or service.

## Blogging

Adding a blog to your business website is a simple procedure for any web developer and the quality and customization options from the big payers such as Wordspace and Blogger leaves very little need to develop your own platform.

A blog will allow you to produce articles, presenting news and comment about your business and its operations. Blogging helps to develop brand building and may provide you with competitive advantage..

## Market places

Market places such as Ebay can be very useful. Although initially conceived as a site where individuals can buy and sell, it now has a facility for professional sellers. Ebay and Amazon in the UK, and Priceminister and Play in Europe, among a few others, provide online business the opportunity to enjoy a worldwide audience by listing your products or services and offering them to their enormous customer base. By paying a listing fee, or a monthly fee plus a share or percentage of the sale price, your business can gain enormous reach within a very short time.

To make it easy for businesses to sell via marketplace sites, these online sellers offer a route to professional sellers to be able to bulk load their products. This is achieved through XML, CSV or through an online portal. There will be some work involved on your side adapting your product database to the platforms particular product classification rules, but once that is done, it is usually a straightforward process loading your products.

The listing fee, commission on sale and other fees can tend to be high if you are selling low margin items. However, the sheer size of the audience can make it worthwhile. As with many other things, it is a case of trying it, dipping your toe in the water and see whether it is worth carrying on.

***************

# Chapter 10

## Keeping the Customer Happy-Customer Service

With any business, managing customer relationships is vitally important. When they have purchased a good, or goods or services, the customer likes to feel valued and treated well. If they do, they themselves will come back to your site and will recommend your business to others.

Your business will have a policy which will promise a level of service delivery. You might promise next day delivery, you might offer a free gift with goods and services. Make sure that you run your business in line with your policy. Don't get sloppy. Remember that you will be up against competition. The way for you to keep customers and develop your customer base is for you to keep them satisfied. It doesn't take long for word to get about that your business fails to deliver.

### Make sure that people can access your business

This may sound obvious. If people cannot access your business, or your business site for some reason then you haven't got a business.

The relationship with a customer begins from them becoming aware of your business and, particularly if you are an online business, your website, and then from the first click which gives them access to your site. Your homepage has to be clear and uncluttered and also needs to be clear and straightforward enabling the potential customer to see the product and go through to the ordering page and buy.

Another very important aspect of your business is the ease of communication with you. For example, I use Google and am a member of their partner programme and they are absolutely impossible to contact. They used to have a support line but that is now gone and they cannot be contacted personally. I ended up writing to their headquarters in California with my grievance. This experience fostered within me the feeling that I no longer wish to deal with them. They have become faceless and anonymous. Make very sure that this is not the case with your business. Ensure that there is an address and telephone number as well as an email so that customers can phone you up. This is most important. It is also useful to have a frequently asked questions page so that people can find answers without contacting you personally.

## Terms and conditions

Any business offline or online, business will have, or should have, a terms and conditions page. Most users, when they purchase something, will click the little box to state that they have read and understood the terms and conditions of that business and what it offers. The reality is that most people don't read them as it is boring.

However, as a business owner, the terms and conditions of the business are crucial. Your terms and conditions will outline exactly what is expected of users of the site and what users can expect from the business. You might want to take a look at the terms and conditions of another business and also take legal advice before you formulate yours.

It is very important to have a privacy policy which is, essentially, a document which outlines your policy in respect of what customer information you will collect, and what you plan to do with this information now and in the future.

Customers can be suspicious especially now with the rise of online identity theft and they will need reassurance. When you create your privacy policy you will need to be very clear about what you intend to do with customer's information. In all likelihood this will be retained for your own use and you won't be doing anything with it. Having thought this through then you should make sure that this is enshrined in a privacy policy and put up onto your site. This will go a long way to reassuring customers.

## Customer service

There is a lot to customer service, over and above offering a phone number and address on the website. You will need to manage the customers who phone you up. Online business, as with all business, will have a fairly significant rate of calls from customers wanting to know where the order is, reporting damage or some aspect of the service that has either gone wrong or that they want to chase up.

Your tone with customers must, at all times and without fail, be polite and courteous and helpful, providing answers to problems. You can get some pretty rude people contacting you and it is important that you are polite but firm and answer queries tactfully.

Treating customers well leads to repeat business and also recommendations to others. Before you know it your business becomes well known through word of mouth.

Customer service policies of most business will contain guidelines for the customer to follow, offering 'service promises'. Your customer service policy may typically contain the following:

- Contact details for the customer-this will typically be a phone number and e mail address plus business address.

- A guide to when customers can receive a reply-i.e. within 24 hours of contacting you.

- A promise to remedy problems as soon as possible.

- A promise of compensation if the problem is not solved in a reasonable time.

All of the above, simple though it may be, will give customers confidence in your business.

## Newsletters

You might want to put together a regular newsletter talking about your business, any changes and also what's new in terms of products. You will have a list of customers to whom you can send this out and may also have obtained a mailing list from elsewhere. This newsletter will be physically sent out as opposed to emailed out.

It is important that customers opt in to receive newsletters and this can be ascertained when they first enter your site or buy a product.

## Marketing by email

If you manage an email marketing campaign correctly, this can be a powerful tool in the whole marketing spectrum. As we have seen from the previous chapter traditional marketing techniques are powerful, always have been. However, with the advent of online business, email marketing can be equally powerful.

One big problem with email marketing, and I think that we all know this from experience, is that emails can be treated as just more junk, more spam to be deleted. Indeed, given the content of most email marketing, it is no surprise. Watches from Switzerland, Viagra from India, you name it. There is one common denominator here: no one touches them with a barge pole.

The first thing that you need to consider is, 'what email addresses can you use? Unless people opt in to specifically receive your e mail shots then you cannot use their address. This is because data protection laws apply to the internet. We all know that this doesn't stop legions of people sending us spam emails. However, in order to stay on the right side of the law, and to maintain the integrity of your business, you need to respect people's right to privacy. Again, on your site you will have a tick box which gives people the choice to opt in or out.

When sending out emails you need to selectively target the recipients. You will need to ensure that those who receive your emails will be interested in buying your products. This means that of all the people or business on your list, you will need to break them down into clusters to identify the ones that you want to contact at any given time and with which product or service.

## Content of the email

This is most important and should reflect the overall tone and content of your business. With email marketing, you need to get the message across quickly and effectively. You will need to ensure that:

- The specific product, promotion or service is highlighted at the outset
- How the user will benefit from this product or service
- What you expect the reader of the email to do next.

You will need to design the email content to reflect the product, service or promotion. You will also have to take time and care to ensure that the benefit to the user is highlighted clearly. The benefit could be simply price or a whole host of other benefits such as legal updates, free offers to festivals and so on. Be clear and you will catch the potential customer's eye.

Finally, make sure that it is easy for the customers to move to the next step. If they need to click on a link make this obvious and provide the link. If you require a from completed keep questions to a minimum so as not to bore the person involved.

## Testing your own service-Mystery shopping
Having developed your business and designed your site and spent a lot of time, effort and money putting all of the aspects together you might

occasionally want to test it all yourself to see if it stands up to scrutiny and to see if your business is delivering what it says. You can do this through the medium of mystery shopping.

Mystery shopping is usually associated with big business, which will send someone to one of their branches, for example, and become a customer and report back on the whole experience. Assuming that this book is being read by the smaller business person, then it might not seem so relevant.

However, you can still employ someone who is either an additional staff member or someone from outside, to go through the whole experience and come back to you with any criticisms. This person will start by clicking onto your site, reading the content, ordering, reading the privacy policy and your customer service policy, opting in for further information, ordering a good, contacting you with a query and contacting you with post-delivery feedback.

This will prove invaluable to you in ironing out any problems or perceived problems with your business. As your business grows bigger then it will become easier to employ a mystery shopper without the knowledge of staff making the experience more plausible.

************

# Chapter 11.

## More about Developing an Online Business

Without a doubt, the ascendancy of online businesses, internet based businesses, has taken the business world by storm over the last ten years or so. Indeed, more and more people are purchasing their goods online, to the overall detriment of the high street.

At the outset, there was a proliferation of such businesses that culminated in the celebrated dot.com boom. During this period, investors behaved as people do during a housing market surge, or some other spiral, they became irrational and threw their money at anything with a dot.com beside it.

What happened after that is a mirror image of what happens after every economic bubble bursts, many of them went to the wall. A few lucky survivors, such as lastminute.com trimmed their sails and are still around.

As we have discussed, the absolute key to any online business, as it is with any type of business, online or not, is the development of a clear and straightforward plan, one that will carry you through all the steps from inception to completion. The identification of your business, what it is you are supplying, goods or services and how you are going to supply them, how you are going to finance the business and how you are going to get paid, this is the bread and butter and must be clear at the outset.

You also need to remember that your online business, because it is internet based, will cross boundaries and may not necessarily be restricted to the UK. This will depend very much on what you are offering for sale.

## Online v traditional business

As we saw in chapter 1, there are a number of advantages to setting up an online business as opposed to a traditional business:

- Online is relatively inexpensive to create and maintain a presence

- There is an opportunity, because of the worldwide nature of the web, to attract a wider audience and a geographically targeted audience.

However, although all of the ingredients necessary for a traditional business are also necessary for an online business, there are fundamental differences.

## Defining your business-identifying Unique Selling Points (USP's)

Essentially, as the owner of a business, you will be selling products or services online. The products or services that you offer are, usually, already available in a traditional form, on the high street, in one way or another. You can be offering books, holidays, furniture, plumbing supplies, white goods, building services, you name it, the list is endless. You have chosen to sell your product or service online. You will need a good website, which is your shop front, excellent sales and marketing

96

and excellent customer service. However, how you define your business as being different to all other businesses, particularly online businesses, in the shape of Unique Selling Points, is what will ultimately give your business the edge over competition.

Even if there are hundreds of competitors selling the same or similar product, and even if they are more established than you and have built up a brand recognition, your business will gain customers if you can clearly identify the USP's that differentiate your business from the rest. An example of Unique Selling Points may be:

- You offer the product cheaper than the rest or offer free postage, some aspect that can immediately draw in the customer. Price isn't everything but it does help
- Generous payment terms for customers
- Money back guarantee
- Experienced staff
- Many years experience of business before selling online

Whatever your USP this needs to be clearly identified and advertised. It could be that your USP's are not immediately apparent at the outset of your business but, as time goes on, and you study the competition more will become apparent.

## The technical side

As an online business, your web presence is of vital importance. This requires creating and maintaining the site. This will involve front-end development, i.e. creating the shop front online, database development, systems administration and general administration.

You, or someone that you are working with, will require the skills to maintain the shopping portal, the website. If you don't have the requisite skills then you will need to hire them in. This costs money so it is vitally important that you have a clear brief for the experts to work from. It is also vitally important that you own the final product and remain in control. In short, develop a clear and unambiguous relationship with the web designers and systems administrators. If you get the design of your site wrong and it doesn't attract customers then there is no real future.

## The legal aspects of an online business

As with every operation there are legal implications for you and your business. This impacts on what you sell and where you sell it. You should seek legal advice when embarking on an online business, as although the law may appear straightforward it sometimes isn't.

As a bare minimum you need to display website terms and conditions and also your privacy policy. If you intend to sell products outside of the United Kingdom then you need to be aware of any government restrictions, by the way of embargoes and also any licenses you may need depending on territories that you want to sell in, particularly in relation to consumer electronics and entertainment or media products. Don't just go entering these markets without researching requirements. Take legal advice. It might cost you but it is money well spent and should be treated as a start-up cost.

## Setting up Your Business Online

If you don't have the technical expertise to create your own website, and most people don't, then you will need to have a very clear idea of what it is you are trying to create and find someone to work with. You will also have to have a clear idea of what your initial budget is for your website.

There are certain questions that you need to ask, such as:

- Do you know what it is that you require from your website?
- How many products will you be offering?
- What will be the ongoing maintenance requirements of the site, will you want to regularly change the appearance of the site?
- Who exactly are you trying to target with your site?

Website developers won't really be interested in your longer term business plan but will require a well worked out brief. It is essential that you look at websites selling similar content so you can get an idea of what it is you are trying to achieve.

As a start you should write down the following:

- How many pages will your site require? In the first instance you don't need to worry about the pages that display products as these will be dynamically created as the site is developed. Of more importance is the number of static pages, such as 'contact us' 'about us' privacy policy and so on. When you have identified the static pages you are well on the way to creating an initial sitemap.
- Note down the content and structure of the site, what is it that your site will contain, is it just text and images or will there be downloads, video clips and review sections etc.? By identifying this you will assist the developer in deciding on the most suitable technology for the site.

- Future content management. Who will do this in the future and how often will it need to be modified?
- Marketing. You will need to have an idea of which on and offline marketing channels you plan to use in conjunction with the business, so your developer can build in the functionality at the outset to allow this to happen in the future.
- Website monitoring. You will almost certainly want to know how well your site is performing in terms of number of visitors and sales. You will also want to know where the traffic is coming from. Make allowances to integrate tools such as Google Analytics into the site. If you are planning an e-commerce store, you will want more detailed financial reporting, not only basic sales information but also tools to manage returns, stock levels, VAT and so on.

## Choosing a web developer

It's true to say that there are now literally thousands of website developers around, ranging from those with very little knowledge, they may have completed a basic course, to the more technically proficient and experienced. It is therefore important, given the importance of getting it right at the outset, to carry out research on a number of developers. You will want to look carefully at the areas listed below.

## Experience

You will want to assess how long the developer has been operating and what their track record is, what they have developed in the past. It would be a wise move to choose a developer who has had experience of developing websites for similar companies and therefore knows the requirements. An experienced developer will be able to discuss various technology options with you and the good and bad points associated with each.

## Development skills and knowledge

It is likely that the developer that you are employing will have a far greater knowledge of web technology than you. However, you can ask such questions as- do they intend to build the website from scratch, or are they using an 'off the shelf' model, i.e. one that has been developed or partially developed for someone else? If you are planning to sell products online then you will want to know their views on e-commerce/shopping basket solutions, whether they recommend PayPal or Worldpay for example can they set up a facility to pay by credit card and also will there be a basic content management system which will allow you or your staff to edit and delete items on the site without continuous recourse to the developer?

## References from other clients

Any web developer worth his or her salt will not object to you asking other clients about the performance of the developer. As the investment in a website is one of the early major investments then it is of the utmost importance that some form of reference is taken up.

## Future project management

You will want to ensure that the chosen developer explains how the process of developing the site works. You will need to ensure that it is brought in well within time and budget. Basic questions are: how often will you be informed of progress, who your contacts are and how can they be reached. In addition, you will need to ascertain how flexible the developer is if you want to add or subtract a feature to the website half way through development.

There are other aspects of development that you need to take on board, such as where the developer is based, how accessible they are, what are their education and qualifications and also, vitally, can you get on with them. You will have fairly close contact with the developer and you need to ensure that you have a good personal relationship with them. Communication is everything!

## Website security and payment methods

Website security, and particularly security involving the taking of money over your site, for products and services, means having a legal responsibility to protect customer data. The worst case is someone's personal information being abstracted from your site and ending up in the hands of scammers. This has been a major headache for online business for a long time now.

Although in the main, regular internet connections between the user and the web are secure, because it doesn't place the user at risk, you will need to integrate a Secure Sockets layer for protection which will give protection and provides a safe way for client and server to communicate. Essentially, SSL protocol encrypts the data being sent over the net between client and server which renders it useless to any third party. You know your connection to a website is secure when the web address begins with https:// and you might also, on some browsers notice a closed padlock icon. The SSL can be added to the site by your developer without difficulty. Ordinarily, the vast majority of your website will be accessed in the normal way until you reach the point when the user wishes to pay for goods. It is very wise to indicate on your site that you employ SSL, which will give customers confidence to carry out their transactions and to pass on their personal payment details. Failure to indicate that the method is secure can cost you sales, simply because we are living in a time of heightened awareness of scamming.

## Payment methods over the web

As indicated, there are a number of ways to facilitate payment over the web. The chosen method will need to be integrated by the designer. To enable online payment you will need to set up a payment gateway and a merchant account. However, as we will see, there are several ways, some simpler than others to set up a gateway. Payment gateways are an interface between your website, and the banks/card issuers around the world. There are a large number of providers and you can choose to work with a specialist provider or your own bank. Your own bank will invariably be happy to set up this gateway with you. You will need to look at the various methods on offer and compare the fees. Some charge more than others. Most providers will charge on a scale, meaning that the more transactions the cheaper it becomes. This may not be the best deal for a start up business, as your initial traffic and sales will be slow to build up. A merchant account is a depository into which funds you receive from online payments are made. This is one option. However, whichever option you choose, the process works as follows:

Step 1. Customer enters card details on your website.

Step 2. The card is authenticated-the details are sent via your payment gateway, to the card issuer. If the card details cannot be verified then the card will be declined.

Step 3. Payment authorization-The issuing bank checks that the cardholder's details are correct and that there are enough funds to cover the transaction and that the card hasn't been reported lost or stolen. Once all checks are carried out then an instruction is sent to the bank to debit funds.

Step 4. Payment settlement-your account is credited within a few days of the actual transaction.

Arguably the most popular payment method which can easily be integrated into your site is PayPal. It provides a simple method for payment and the costs are low, particularly for a new business. there are other payment methods similar to PayPal which can be explored on the web.

## The process of ordering

We will be discussing the creation of content on your site in the chapter on marketing, however, at this stage it is essential to ensure that once customers have chosen a product or service then they can actually complete the ordering process, and that it is an easy path. I know from my own experience that a process that is too long-winded can work against the business and can lose you sales.

## Ensure that the A-Z process is simple

Part of an integrated system for purchasing over a website is what is known as the 'shopping basket'. I am sure that you will have seen this on Amazon or similar sites. You are invited to place items in a shopping trolley before checkout. This gives the feeling that you are in an actual store. This is known as the order pipeline  and is the process and the number of pages that a consumer must navigate before the completion of the sale. It is important that the order pipeline has as few stages as possible so that the customer doesn't become frustrated. Therefore, you need to define what details are essential to complete the order and what information can be captured at a later date.

## Exploiting Your Sites Potential-Making additional Money from Your Site

Once you have set your website up, you can start thinking about making money from day one. You can earn money from activities quite apart from your mainstream business.

One of the main areas for generating extra revenue is that of advertising. Choosing to display advertising on your website is a good way to earn extra money. Basically, users of your site will see advertising and if they like what they see then they will click on the advert. This is what generates the money, each click earns you money, the amount varying with the advertiser. However, for this to work you must have enough traffic on your site to bring in potential 'clickers'

The problem with advertising is that it can serve to cheapen a site. Typically, people go over the top when setting up banner adverts on their site and the end result is that there are scores of adverts selling products which have little or nothing to do with the core product that you sell. This will serve as a distraction and people will rapidly leave your site.

For example, your business might be publishing and related industries. To have your website plastered with ads for car insurance and holidays in the sun would be counterproductive. However, to advertise the consumer magazine 'Which' would be a far better fit. Therefore, you need to give a lot of thought to what adverts you want on your site, if you want to maintain the integrity of your site.

Signing up with Google Adsense is relatively simple as is the integration into your site. You can use Google's back office tools to select the type of advertising that you want.

Display, or banner ads usually use the CPC (cost per click) or CPM (cost per thousand) model. Basically, you get paid for every click or every thousand clicks.

You need to keep grounded about the potential money you might earn from this, as the big earners are of course Google, Facebook and the like. Also, take a look at your own behaviour. When you surf the web, alight on sites, how many times do you actually click on adverts.

The main advice to you is that when deciding to place adverts on your site, don't go mad in the hope of earning money, as this can ruin your site, cheapen it and confuse the user. Also, the dreamed of riches from placing ads can be pie in the sky! Concentrate on your core business, selling your product or service to the public and treat any revenues from advertising as a secondary minor source of revenue.

## Selling third party products

In addition to advertising, the web offers a wide variety of potential revenue streams. Even if your business sells specialist products and you would rather not plaster your site with advertising there are a number of digital products that you can promote on your site. For example, organizations such as CLICKBANK www.clickbank.com have many thousands of products that you can promote. The following are some of the features:

- Commissions are on a sliding scale, some offering up to 75% per sale
- There is an opportunity to earn ongoing revenue from subscription based products
- You can obtain full back-office statistics to help you manage the process.

You should visit their website, outlined above, for more information. This may or may not be for you but it is another opportunity to maximise revenue.

## Affiliation

Affiliation is easy to implement both as an advertiser (those who want others to help them sell their product or service and pay a commission) or alternatively as a publisher where you help sell the goods and services of others and earn a commission. It can be, although again be realistic, a very good way of generating revenue online without too much involvement. Basically, you are a conduit for traffic for your chosen affiliate/partner and you make money earning a commission every time one of your visitors clicks on a link or interacts with your advertiser's site through your site.

Many people might choose to work with a large organisation such as Amazon, become an Amazon Associate, If you don't want to work with a single provider, or you don't want to promote the products that a particular organisation sells then you can investigate Affiliation Networks.

## Affiliate Networks

Affiliate networks are big business. They match advertisers with publishers (companies selling with those who will promote goods). Affiliate networks vary in size, reputation and ability to attract highest profile advertisers and publishers. The more successful networks will charge advertisers a fee to join the programme and more often than not a monthly fee for managing the account. It is usually free to become a publisher and that's why it can prove a lucrative earner for your site. Affiliate networks make their money from the set up and monthly fees paid by advertisers along with a commission of the total revenue generated for the client.

## Product feeds

Accepting a product feed from an advertiser can require some development work but what this gives you is the ability to display as many or as few products as you wish to from an advertisers website. For example, if your business is that of publishing you can promote books and magazines, with product names, descriptions and pricing etc. What you are essentially doing is to promote someone else's products straight from their site. Product feeds are a very effective way to build up a large website quickly. It is an effective way to sell a product online without the risk. www.productfeed.org is a useful website to visit.

## Supplying Goods and Services-The Supply Chain

One of the most important elements of any business is making sure that it can provide goods, good quality goods, on time.

## Local suppliers

If you are selling physical goods, finding a local supplier will be a great advantage. The closer to home the supplier then the greater control that you will have. Local can mean anywhere within the UK. Local products mean reduced costs, lower freight charges, free local delivery or self-service pick up options. This will all help to save money. Also, local suppliers mean better stock management in that local suppliers can often hold onto stock until consignment.

## Buying from abroad

Many products can be sourced cheaply from abroad, particularly from places such as China. Buying products from countries such as these will no doubt help to improve your profitability in the long run. However, unless you have the time to go to the relevant country and purchase goods, and you are fully aware of the tax implications, then all sorts of risks are presented. Even if you cannot find the time or money to visit a potential trading partner abroad, there are many online trading platforms offering a huge range of potential suppliers and goods, (Business-to-Business platforms). Many charge businesses to advertise their contact details and place descriptions of their products, others will charge buyers a membership fee to gain access to contact details, some others charge a commission. A few such trading platforms are:

- www.alibaba.com
- www.tradekey.com
- www.globalsources.com
- www.diytrade.com

There are many more. Eventually you will want to meet suppliers and forge a relationship. There is nothing better than this to ensure confidence and security and to discuss trade terms.

## Choosing a supplier of goods

You should keep all the data that you receive from the various potential suppliers. The name of the game is competition. For instance, when you have set up your business and are ready to go, you might eventually run into problems with your suppliers for a variety of reasons, price, service delivery, customer care and so on, and may want to switch supplier. You should build up a data bank of suppliers so that you are in a position to move if necessary.

## Managing the suppliers

Maintaining good relations with your suppliers is as important as managing your customers. Suppliers are very important, without them you don't really have a business. Managing suppliers well is wholly dependent on how well you communicate with them. There are many instances of relationships starting off well and then something goes wrong and the whole pack of cards collapses. The essence of good management is face-to-face communication. Find time to meet on a regular basis with your suppliers. Remember they have their own pressures too, so sit down and talk about any problems that may arise. That goes a long way.

## Organising payment terms

With a new business, it is highly unlikely that you will be given immediate credit by suppliers. Even if you are known personally to the supplier from a previous life, the first order will have to be paid up front. However, once you have a history with a supplier, once you have maintained regular payments, then it is likely that you will be given time to pay. Usually, 30 days from invoice date is the norm. The same goes with your business bank account. In the first instance it is very unlikely that you will be given generous business overdraft terms. Again, it will be dependent on your track record. your relationship with a supplier begins from the word go, when you place your first order. Make sure that the account information that they have is correct, the billing address, delivery address, contact numbers and email address, along with VAT number if applicable and payment terms.

When you receive an order be rigorous and check that the contents are what you ordered and that the quantity is correct. Mistakes can happen and they should be rectified at the outset otherwise problems can arise.

## Breaking off relationships with a supplier

No matter how good the relationship is with your supplier, there may come a time when you will need to sever ties. It may be that things started to go wrong and they have progressively got worse. There could have been a change of personnel and the time and effort that has been expended building up a relationship has all gone out of the window. Whatever, it is time to switch.

Once you have found a replacement supplier then you will need to notify your existing supplier that you no longer require their services and that all outstanding invoices will be paid. Although feelings may have been hurt, business comes first. It is highly likely that you will have warned your supplier beforehand of problems so it may not come as a shock.

## Stock control

The type of business that you run and the type of goods that you provide, will determine the level of stock control that will be required. If someone is ordering from you and you order the goods from someone else and they are delivered direct to the buyer's door then the whole process of stock control is simple. However, if you are buying goods in bulk at one price and delivering direct to the customer yourself then this will require a different system. To run your e-commerce store smoothly from the outset, you will need to make sure that you have the correct tools to do this.

## Bar code printer

Depending on the type of products that you are planning to sell and how far up the supply chain you are sourcing your products, you will need to obtain a bar code printer. Bar codes make light work of stock management and a bar code printer will prove invaluable if you need to label your product.

## Bar code scanners

To assist you in both receiving and picking and packing customer orders, a barcode scanner will be most useful. Setting up your back office will take time initially as you assign each and every product a bar code but once done then stock can move quickly into and out of the warehouse.

## Stock management systems

In the first instance, a simple spreadsheet might suffice to keep accurate records of stock movement. However, as your business grows and becomes more complex it is likely that you will need a more sophisticated system. There are a number of systems around that might be suitable and if you require a demonstration it is likely that a company would be willing to do this for you.

## Invoicing customers

Controlling cash flow is the lifeblood of any business. Spending money is easy but getting the money in can be a different story. It is your legal obligation to provide customers with an invoice and a receipt along with every order shipped. Invoices can detail numerous orders on one sheet. The invoice must contain basic details, such as your company address and your registration details plus VAT number if applicable. The customer's order must be fully outlined and also the price that they have paid. Whilst all of this sounds obvious it is amazing how many companies send out inadequate invoices which are then not paid.

In addition, it goes without saying that invoices must be tracked and late payers contacted immediately. Strong credit control is vitally important. Again, it is amazing how many companies send out invoices then lose track of them doing nothing about them until they accidentally discover, or their accountant discovers, that they haven't been paid.

## The storage of stock

If you are in a position where you have to store stock before delivery then there are a few basic rules that you should observe:

- Make sure that where you store your stock is appropriate-i.e. it is dry and clean and suits the goods that you plan to store. Any damage to goods once delivered from the original supplier to you will be down to you

- Make sure that the storage is secure and protected from fire or theft-ensure adequate alarms and also current insurance is in place
- Make sure that you have adequate systems in place to check goods received. If the incorrect number of goods arrives, or there is damage this should be dealt with then and there
- Carry out regular stock takes. This becomes more important as the business grows.
- Make sure that stock is stored in a logical and ordered way. Have clearly numbered areas where specific stock resides so it can be found easily

## Picking and packing stock

In the first instance, the picking of stock may not be a great problem as your business will probably be small. However, it is when it grows that it can become more complex.

The following are tips for you when organising the selection of stock:

- You should have a picking list which enables you to go straight to the item you want. This will save time and effort
- Ensure that an invoice/receipt is sent with every order
- If you don't have all the items when packing the order notify the customer straight away
- Ensure items are well packaged to avoid damage

## Delivery of items

This is always a contentious area. My own experience of delivery has been that, no matter how much companies put into promoting the product and making all sorts of promises, the end link in the chain, delivery of items, lets them down. There is nothing worse than a surly delivery driver virtually throwing the goods at you or refusing to carry goods up the stairs or whatever. In short, rudeness and inflexibility. I hasten to add that this isn't true across the board but it is in many cases. Given that everything about online shopping should be about convenience, including delivery, then it is important to choose the right partner, which could be Royal Mail, FedEx or any one of the delivery companies. Usually, you would sign a deal with one or other that can guarantee price and also provide some sort of track record when it comes to delivery.

Courier companies will usually offer attractive rates for volume deliveries so it will be up to you to negotiate the appropriate contract. You should look for the following:

- Courier companies who will collect from your address and can give specified times for delivery
- Some companies will also handle returns as part of the contract, make sure that this is in your contract
- International orders are slightly different-they must have a customs statement from your company clearly marked on the outside of the package which includes a description of the contents. You can check with www.hmrc.gov.uk for more information.

## Returns

There are a number of reasons why returns are made: incorrect goods sent to the customer, damaged goods or customer changes his or her mind. Whatever the reason, returns happen and have to be dealt with. The following are useful tips when dealing with returns:

- When the good is returned check the damage, if damage is alleged, to see whether this is down to you or to the manufacturer
- Make sure you keep an accurate record of returns and adjust stock accordingly
- Acknowledge that you have received the return-this is good customer service and might encourage the customer to buy again
- Keep an eye of people who buy and return on a regular basis-this can happen, especially with items such as DVD's, which can be copied. After a while you can sort out those who are operating this kind of scam.

***************

## Useful Addresses

Advertising Association
7th Floor North
Artillery House
1-19 Artillery Row
London SW1P 1RT
020 7340 1100
www.adasocc.org

Advisory Conciliation and
Arbitration Service (ACAS)
Customer helpline 0300 123 1100
www.acas.org.uk

British Chambers of Commerce
65 Petty France
London
SW1H 9EU
020 7654 5800
www.britishchambers.org

BNR Business Names Registration
Somerset House
Temple Street
6070 Birmingham Business Park
B37 7BF
Email: sales@start.biz
Tel  0121 678 9000

British Franchising Association,
Centurion Court
85F Park Drive
Milton Park
Abingdon
OX14 4RY
www.thebfa.org.uk
01235 820470

British Venture Capital Association
5th Floor east
Chancery House
53-64 Chancery lane
London WC2 1QS
0207 492 0400
www.bvca.co.uk

Business in the Community
137 Shepherdess Walk
London N1 7RQ
Tel 0207 566 8650
www.bitc.co.uk

The Chartered Institute of
Patent Attorneys
95 Chancery Lane
London WC2A 1DT
Tel 0207 405 9450
www.cipa.org.uk

Chartered Institute of Marketing
Moor Hall
Cookham
Maidenhead
Berkshire
SL6 9QH
01628 427 120
www.cim.co.uk

Companies Registration Office
Companies House
Crown Way
Cardiff
CF4 3UZ
www.companieshouse.gov.uk

Confederation of British
Industry (CBI)
Cannon Place
78 Cannon Street
London EC4 6HN
Tel 0207 379 7400
www.cbi.org.uk

Department for Business, Innovation and skills
www.bis.gov.uk
0207 215 5000

Federation of
Small Businesses
Sir Frank Whittle Way
Blackpool Business Park
Blackpool
FY4 2FE
Tel 0808 2020 888
www.fsb.org.uk

Forum of Private Business
https://fpb.org
0845 130 1722

Grants and Funding Information
www.grantsnet.co.uk
www.j4b.co.uk

Health and Safety Executive
Rose Court
2 Southwark B0ridge
London
SE1 9HS
www.hse.gov.uk

Institute of Trade Mark Attorneys
5th Floor
Outer Temple
222-225 Strand
London
WC2R 1BA

020 7101 6090
www.itma.org.uk

Intellectual Property Office
0300 300 2000
Email enquiries@ipo.gov.uk

National Enterprise Network
Acorn House
381 Midsummer Boulevard
Milton keynes
MK9 3HP
01908 605130
www.nationalenterprisenetwork.org

Scottish Enterprise
Atrium Court
50 Waterloo Street
Glasgow G2 6HQ
Tel 0845 607 8787
www.scottish-enterprise.com

UK Trade and Investment
1 Victoria Street
London
SW1H OET
0845 539 049

Welsh Development Agency (WDA)
01443 845500

## Online Business-Useful addresses

## Business Networks & advice

---

Business Link: www.businesslink.gov.uk
Chamber of Commerce: www.britishchambers.org.uk
Federation of Small Businesses: www.fsb.org.uk
Business Gateway: www.bgateway.com
StartUps. co.uk: www.startups.co.uk
Linked In: www.linkedin.com
xing: www.xing.com

---

## Paid Search/PPC
www.google.com/adwords
http://adcenter.microsoft.com
http://advertisingcentral.yahoo.com

---

## Company Formation Specialists
www.completeformations.co.uk
www.companiesmadesimple.com

---

## Venture Capital & Business Angels
USAvFinance: www.vfinance.com

## Domain Names& HOSTING
(USA) www.godaddy.com

(UK)  www.123-reg.co.uk

---

Online Marketplaces
Amazon.com:  www.amazon.com
Play.com  www.play.com
eBay  www.ebay.com

---

Email Marketing Platform
www.cheetamail.com
www.dotmailer.co.uk
www.emaildem.com

---

Internet Marketing Agencies
Coast Digital:  www.coastdigital.co.uk
Conver247:  www.convert247.com
Eleven Marketing:  www.11marketing.com

---

Internet E-Commerce Platform
http://www.magento.com
http://www.oscommerce.com
http://zencart.com
http://virtuemart.net
http://wwwdashcommerce.org

---

Online Payment Systems & Gateways
Patpal:  www.paypal.com

Nochex: www.nochex.com
WorldPay: www.worldpay.com

---

Internet Industry Research
www.mintel.com

---

Social Media
www.delicious.com
http://digg.com
www.facebook.com
www.reddit.com
www.stumbleupon.com
http://technorati.com
www.twitter.com
www.linkedin.com

***************

# Index

*************

Appendix 1-Sample Business Plan

The following pages represent the basis for your business plan and the various sections relate to the sections of the book. If there are parts which you do not feel are relevant to your business, then you should ignore them.

You should construct your own business plan using the following as a guide. By referring to the book and also to the details of your own business you should be in a position to formulate your own plan which will be the complete document for your use, particularly for presentation to your bank manager or to other parties. Remember, it has been stressed throughout the book that an impressive business plan goes a long way towards developing your business and raising the necessary funds to go forward.

Your Business Plan

Name of business

_____

Address_____

_____

Telephone
Number_____

Sole Trader_____    Partnership_____    Franchise___    Limited Company_____

Start up date_____
Type Business_____

Planning ahead

My ultimate goal is

_____

_____

_____

_____

I expect to achieve the following over the next few years

Year
1_____

_____

Year
2_____

_____

Year
3_____

_____

Marketing

I have identified my market
as_____

_____

_____

_____

_____

_____

_____

My customers may be described

as_____

_____

_____

_____

_____

_____

_____

_____

_____

Product comparison table

|  | My Product | Competitor A | Competitor B |
|---|---|---|---|
| Price |  |  |  |
| Quality |  |  |  |
| Availability |  |  |  |
| Customers |  |  |  |
| Staff Skills |  |  |  |

Reputation

---

Advertising

---

Delivery

---

Location

---

Special Offers

---

After Sales Service

---

My product is special because

_____

_____

_____

_____

_____

_____

The main advantages of my product over my competitors are

_____

_____

_____

_____

_____Pricing

Calculating your break even point

Personal Drawings

_____

_____

National Insurance

_____

_____

Tax

_____

_____

Stationary

_____

_____

Advertising

_____

_____


Telephone

_____

_____

Rent and Rates

_____

_____

Heating and Lighting

_____

Vehicle Depreciation

_____

_____

Petrol

_____

_____

Servicing

_____

_____

Road Tax Fund

_____

_____

Insurance

_____

_____

Business Insurance

_____

_____

Bad Debts

_____

_____

Premises
My business will be located at

_____

_____

_____

_____

_____

Because

_____

_____

_____

_____

_____

_____

Details of my lease/licence/rent/rate/next rent review

_____

_____

_____

_____

_____

_____

Details of key staff (if any

Name_____

_____

Position_____

_____

Address_____

Age_____

_____

Qualifications_____

_____

_____

Relevant work experience

_____

_____

_____

_____

_____

_____

Present
Income_____

_____

Repeat as necessary

I will need to buy in the following skills during the first two years

_____

_____

_____

_____

_____

I estimate the cost of employing people or buying any services I may need in the first two years

| Number of people | Job Function | Monthly Cost | Annual cost |
| --- | --- | --- | --- |

My personal Details
Name

Address

_____

_____

_____

_____

_____

Telephone
(home)_____

_____

Telephone
(work)_____

_____

Qualifications_____

_____

_____

_____

_____

_____

Date of
Birth_____

_____

Business experience

_____

_____

_____

_____

_____

_____

Courses attended

_____

_____

_____

_____

_____

_____

Book-keeping

I intend to keep the following records
(which will be kept up to date by myself/book-keeper/accountant)

_____

_____

Other

Accountant

_____

_____

Address

_____

_____

Telephone_____

_____

Solicitor

Address

_____

_____

_____

_____

_____

_____

Telephone_____

_____

VAT Number_____

Insurance Arrangements_____

Raising finance

By reference to my profit and loss and cashflow forecast, I need to borrow

Amount £
_____For

_____

_____

Period

_____

_____

I am investing £

_____

_____

_____

I can offer the following security

_____

_____

_____

_____